Advance Praise for

Hey Buddy

"*Hey Buddy* is a page-turning pursuit of Buddy Holly's legacy and his impact on others in and out of the music industry. It's as American as apple pie and as compelling as Don McLean's legendary hit about The Day the Music Died. Run, don't walk, to your nearest bookstore and get two copies—one for you and another for anyone you know who listens to music."

— James Riordan, *New York Times* bestselling author of *Break on Through: The Life and Death of Jim Morrison*

"Gary Moore's *Hey Buddy* is a touching narrative that chronicles his fascinating journey of discovery into the life and music of Buddy Holly through the spirited performances of John Mueller while endeavoring to explain the profound impact Buddy's musical legacy continues to have more than fifty years after his tragic demise."

— Jacqueline A. Bober, Curator, The Buddy Holly Center

"A rock-and-rollercoaster of a read! Gary Moore's emotional account of his discovery of Buddy Holly and the eye-and-ear-witnesses of Holly's genius is a memorial to the influence of one of rock's true pioneers. You'll 'Rave On' about this unforgettable story!"

— Bill Guertin, longtime vinyl rock-and-roll DJ and the author of *Reality Sells: The 800-Pound Gorilla of Sales*

"We've all had Uncle Charlies in our lives who were fun to be around because they told such great stories; we always wanted to hear more. For me, Gary Moore is the 'Uncle Charlie' of American writers. He is a great storyteller through the written word—and I always want to read more. Now he's done it again with *Hey Buddy*."

— John Skipper, author of *Meredith Willson: The Unsinkable Music Man*

"*Hey Buddy* illustrates the raw power that passion for a topic can have when it grips an unsuspecting writer. Author Gary Moore is not only a gifted storyteller but an accomplished musician and a pilot, and he uses these attributes to provide new and unique insights into Holly's music, his all-too-brief life . . . and his death."

— Bonnie Bartel Latino, author and former columnist for *Stars and Stripes* newspaper–Europe

"Buddy Holly inspired a generation of musical greatness. But in many ways, he was very different from the musicians he inspired in his short life. These differences are what allowed a former rock n roll naysayer to finally come to grips with his musical prejudice. In discovering Buddy, Gary Moore learns as much about himself as he does about a generation of music he had selectively tuned out. *Hey Buddy* allowed me to walk on this journey with him. It is really terrific—sweet, sad, informative, and even patriotic. This is a great read for anyone remotely interested in music and why it does or doesn't make us tick."

— Beth Kenney-Augustine, Emmy award-winning producer

Hey Buddy

In Pursuit of Buddy Holly, My New Buddy John,

and My Lost Decade of Music

Gary W. Moore

SB

Savas Beatie

New York and California

Cataloging-in-Publication Data is available from the Library of Congress.

ISBN 978-1-932714-97-5

05 04 03 02 01 5 4 3 2 1
First edition, first printing

SB

Published by
Savas Beatie LLC
521 Fifth Avenue, Suite 1700
New York, NY 10175

Editorial Offices:

Savas Beatie LLC
P.O. Box 4527
El Dorado Hills, CA 95762
Phone: 916-941-6896
(E-mail) editorial@savasbeatie.com

Savas Beatie titles are available at special discounts for bulk purchases in the United States by corporations, institutions, and other organizations. For more details, please contact Special Sales, P.O. Box 4527, El Dorado Hills, CA 95762, or you may e-mail us at sales@savasbeatie.com, or visit our website at www.savasbeatie.com for additional information.

For Arlene, the love of my life

Buddy Holly, tuning his guitar on a freezer in the kitchen
at the Electric Park Ballroom in Waterloo, Iowa. *Courtesy of Dick Cole*

Contents

Contents (continued)

Contents (continued)

Contents (continued)

"I'm often asked, if Buddy Holly lived, where would the music have taken him? I politely say that they are asking the wrong question. It should be, if Buddy had lived where would he have taken the music?"

— Waylon Jennings

Splooie!

(And only because this book is dedicated to Arlene . . . SUTA!)

Foreword

An Appreciation for The "Pursuit"

In some ways it's a little difficult to write an introduction to a book in which you are quoted and featured in a couple sections. Even for someone with an oversized ego like mine, it presents a challenge. But this fine book is not about me or any of the other people quoted within its pages. We simply banded together in print to talk about the amazing phenomena that was and in many ways still is Buddy Holly. Buddy was a music innovator who influenced countless artists who came after him. He was the force behind the *"Texas radio with the big beat"* that Jim Morrison of The Doors wrote about. Buddy was the creator of that rock-a-billy sound that everyone in the 1960s, including The Beatles and the Rolling Stones, openly borrowed from.

This is a fun book with a sense of humor that is true to both author and subject. Gary Moore has been a friend of mine for a long time. He's a talented writer and if you have experienced his work before, you know he's a lot of fun to read. Gary says some very serious things while poking fun at himself for having the audacity to put them in print. I admire that.

I also understand Gary's passionate interest and deep need to "pursue" Buddy Holly. Some of us are just built that way. When that virus gets inside you there is no cure and there is no choice but to let it follow its course. When I was writing *Break on Through*, a biography of Jim Morrison, I had no alternative but to eat, sleep, dream, and study the man and his life and music. Many writers personally caught up in their subject matter experience this roller coaster ride of emotion. It is all-consuming. In some cases it can also be life-changing and awaken something within long dormant or forgotten. In so many ways Gary is the perfect person to revisit the legacy of Buddy Holly. Unraveling its meaning and impact with Gary makes *Hey Buddy* a memorable experience.

Because he died in a tragic plane crash that in itself has become the stuff of legend—*the day the music died*—people forget that Buddy Holly was about so much more than his death. He was a musical pioneer, a consummate performer, and a dedicated family man. He was also a man of faith. Like Buddy, I've had my ups and downs but when all is said and done, I know that being true to my Creator is the ultimate goal. Buddy knew that, too.

I think *Hey Buddy* will fill in the shadows surrounding the myth of Buddy Holly and portray him as not only a legend but a good hardworking young man of flesh and blood who tried his best to remain true to his beliefs.

In the end, what greater thing can we do than that?

James Riordan

Author's Note

Whether a curse or a gift (and my opinion on this point changes daily), things often catch my eye, mind, and heart that other people ignore.

I find meaning in lyrics others do not hear, and I find significance in events and issues others feel are meaningless. I never know when it's going to strike deep, but when it does, this gift opens doors for me that I feel compelled to pass through. And then the journey begins. . . . On this day, I am grateful for this gift.

Millions of Buddy Holly fans love his music. It raves on all over the world every day, decades after his death. For reasons you will learn on the pages that follow, I never paid any attention to Buddy or his music when I was growing up. As you read, you will soon agree that I am one of the least likely people to write anything about Buddy Holly. But the "gift" tapped me on the shoulder one evening and whispered in my ear. The words seized both my mind and my heart and sent me on a passionate search I will now share with you.

As you probably have already discerned, this is not a Buddy Holly biography or a history of his music. *Hey Buddy* is a personal journey—a search for the meaning of Buddy and how he continues to impact, more than five decades after his horrific and untimely death, the lives of others. In the process, I discovered a part of myself I did not know existed.

*   *   *

There is method to my madness, or at least I like to think so.

Most of what follows is written, as are most books, in third person prose. I wrote most of this after the experience took place, so this is appropriate. In some places, though, it seemed more natural to communicate what was going on in my head as I typed the very words on the page. Given the sort of book this is, I hope it helps you, the reader, to experience some of my journey of discovery as I did, in real time. Not everyone fully understood the first time around.

"Gary, you do realize you are changing your time perspective back and forth from chapter to chapter, right?" asked my agent Tris Coburn.

"Yes, Tris. I do." I replied. Silence. "Tris?"

"Yes?"

"What's a tense?" I laughed. Silence.

Some people just don't fully understand me.

*   *   *

"Gary, I'm afraid you are going to drive your readers bonkers if you switch back and forth like this," warned friend and fellow author Bonnie Bartel Latino.

"Thanks, Bonnie. I'm sure you're right, but I am bonkers. You have read the manuscript? They can join me. I'll appreciate the company."

*   *   *

"What exactly are you doing?" asked my publisher Ted Savas. The worry about his investment in me and my book was apparent in his voice.

"I'm writing from my heart. Sometimes in real time, sometimes not," I replied.

"Oh my God, Gary," he groaned. I know Ted well. When something bothers him, he lifts his right hand and rubs his frowning forehead with his eyes closed. "I don't really care if this is first or third person," he continued. "I think it can work either way," he sighed. "Tell me again why I signed you to write this book?"

"I don't know," I said with a laugh. "Because you are a glutton for punishment, maybe?"

*   *   *

The woman put down the manuscript and looked at me from across the kitchen table. "Then . . . now . . . then . . . now . . . then . . . now. Just pick a time-frame and go with it!" she insisted. I nodded in agreement. "But . . . are you *really* going to admit everything you are thinking and feeling on paper for all your friends—and complete strangers—to read?" she asked. Real horror was written across my wife's face.

I shrugged and smiled back.

*   *   *

With great respect for everyone, I decided to write *Hey Buddy* as I felt it, and now it rests in your hands. Consider yourself warned. Look at it this way: We are on a journey together and at some point along the way we stop together and take a break. During that time we engage in intense and emotional conversations about what is happening right at the moment. I just have to tell you! And then we continue on with the story in a more traditional style. I hope you enjoy it.

*   *   *

There are so many people who helped me with this book, and I am certain I have left some of you out. Please know that I know who you are, and that I appreciate your assistance, your support, and your friendship.

John Mueller is a dynamic performer who, among other impressive accomplishments, portrays Buddy Holly in John's touring recreation of the 1959 Winter Dance Party. John is also an accomplished songwriter whose personal tribute to Holly, "Hey Buddy," stirred my heart and my passions. Thank you, John. Your song touched my heart and stimulated my imagination. Your performance sent me on a journey I have loved. I am much better for having taken it. I would not even pretend to speak for Buddy, but I can only believe that he is also very grateful to you for your touching tribute and all the work you continue to do to keep his music alive. The music did not die on that day, after all. Buddy raves on—and today you are his standard bearer.

Thank you to my friend and Managing Director Theodore P. Savas of Savas Beatie LLC for allowing this book to come to life. Ted took a chance on an unpublished author in 2006 with *Playing with the Enemy: A Baseball Prodigy, a World at War, and a Field of Broken Dreams.* Apparently he didn't learn his lesson because he's published me again. Ted is an Iowan, and maybe like a young girl you will soon read about in these pages, has a little of that "Iowa guilt" about Buddy dying in his home state. After all, Ted grew up just eight miles from where Buddy's life ended. I think Ted feels that working with me is the penance he must pay. Thank you, Ted and everyone at Savas Beatie (especially Marketing Director Sarah Keeney) for your continued faith in me and my work.

I also would like to thank Tris Coburn, my friend and literary agent, for your help and support. Like Ted, Tris took a chance with a first-time author and was willing to do it again. I am grateful, Tris, for your help and guidance.

Tim Duggan has been a good friend for many years. He displayed amazing patience as I searched for the music of my youth. Bestselling author Jim Riordan (aka Levi Storm) has a unique point of view and understanding of the 1960s, and he readily shared them with me. Thank you, Jim for all of your help and support. Thank you also to Stacey Cisneros, Bob Hale, Dick Cole, Tim Milner, Ramona and Gary Tollett, Bobby Vee, Taryn Serwatowski, Keith Mastre, Eddie Weir, and Gary Clevenger for sharing your knowledge, your stories, and your candid feelings with me.

Thank you also to Dick Rodriguez for your brilliant insight into the February 1959 crash. Your decades of experience and willingness to share your thoughts proved invaluable to me.

Bonnie Bartel Latino read an early draft of the manuscript and offered keen perspective and endless encouragement, all of which made this book better than it otherwise would have been.

Veteran reporter and legendary baseball writer John Skipper, who writes for the Globe Gazette in Mason City, Iowa, has been my friend since he mentored me during the writing stage of *Playing with the Enemy*. John was early in his encouragement of this project, and has been very helpful throughout.

Thank you Bill Griggs for your time and attention and for dedicating your life to Buddy's memory. No one could have done it better.

Thank you to the people and leaders of Lubbock, Texas, for the support you provide the Buddy Holly Center and other efforts to recognize and remember Buddy Holly and the Crickets. Curator Jacqueline A. Bober gave (and continues to give) willingly of her time and knowledge. I am deeply grateful for the wonderful day I spent with you and your staff at the Buddy Holly Center.

My two sons, Toby and Travis, continue to be a source of fun and excitement in my life. Watching you grow from boys to men has made me more proud than you can know.

I would like to thank my daughter and son-in-law, Tara Beth and Jeff Leach, for being the people you are and for your love for each other. And thank you for my new grandson Caleb Daniel Leach. I can't wait to put drumsticks in his hands.

Arlene is the love of my life, my best friend, and the woman who in the entire world I admire the most. Thank you for listening to me babble for hours about Buddy Holly, and for taking this journey with me.

Thank you to the hippest mother-in-law in the world, Norma Wurster Wigant Jackson and her husband Bob. Thank you both for introducing me to Buddy's music through John Mueller. But more importantly, thank you Norma for welcoming me into your family for the last thirty-five years and for allowing me to marry your daughter who, in so many ways, is just like you.

Buddy Holly. How do I thank you? Your creativity, your enthusiasm, and your gift of music for generations yet unborn has changed my life as it has affected so many others. I marvel at how you, such a young and humble man, could have such a profound and lasting impact upon the world in such a short time. I am guessing Jesus loves to rock and you are a hit in heaven.

And most importantly, thank you to my Lord and Savior Jesus Christ, who loves and supports me through all my weaknesses and failings.

Chapter 1

Hey, Buddy

"You're kidding," I said to the love of my life when she told me of her plan. "Please, tell me you're kidding."

"No, I'm not kidding and you will do this for my mother," replied Arlene with the finality only she is capable of delivering. After thirty-five years of marriage I have a clear understanding of the few battles I can fight and win. This was not one of them. Her plan was set. We were going to drive more than three hundred miles from our home in Bourbonnais, Illinois, to Independence, Iowa to take my 77-year-old mother-in-law and her husband Bob to "The Winter Dance Party" at the University of Northern Iowa in Cedar Falls.

"What is the Winter Dance Party?" I asked.

"I'm not exactly sure. I think it's a Buddy Holly impersonator," Arlene responded, bending down to take the last plate out of the dishwasher. She turned and faced me. "We're going and you will act like you are delighted to be there." She punctuated the word "delighted" with a wide smile.

Mother-in-law jokes aside, I truly love Norma. Norma Wurster Wigant Jackson is an amazing woman in more ways than I will recount on this page. But so often, just when you think you know someone, they throw you for a loop. In all the decades I have known her I have never heard Norma talk about music, and certainly not Rock & Roll. My mother-in-law is a Buddy Holly fan? Get out of town!

Arlene and Gary Moore. *Author*

I stared at Arlene's broad smile as my mind mulled over what little I knew about Buddy Holly. I knew his name, of course, and that there was a movie about him I hadn't seen. I knew he was a musician. I had a hunch he was dead, killed in a plane crash. In fact, I remembered landing at an airport in Iowa in a private plane many years ago and being told by a kid at the airport that the wreckage of Holly's plane was hidden away in a local hangar. I remember doubting it at the time, not really caring one way or the other. I was not a fan of Holly or Rock & Roll, and I had no intention of becoming one.

"Okay. I'll do it for your mom, but I'm going to hate it."

The following day I arrived at my office to meet with Tim Duggan, a good friend and business associate. "I'm going to see Buddy Holly," I offered in passing as I pulled my laptop from its case.

"Thought he was dead," Tim responded casually without bothering to look up from whatever he was reading on his own computer.

"Yeah, I'm pretty sure he is."

Tim looked up. "Then how are you going to see him?" He seemed confused.

"I'm going to see an impersonator."

"I didn't know you were a fan." Tim said. He lowered his eyes and began reading again. He was already losing interest in the conversation.

"No. Not me. Believe it or not, my mother-in-law is."

That got his attention. Tim looked up again. "How old is she?"

"Seventy-seven."

Tim stared at me for several seconds before replying. "Okay. Well, that makes sense. The day the music died was what? 1959?" He paused again. "So she was . . . twenty-six or so when Holly crashed. Of course she would be a fan. Everyone under thirty was a fan."

"Excuse me? The day the music died?" I had no idea what Tim was talking about.

"Get outta here!" Tim answered with a skeptical look on his face. "You know, "American Pie." The day the music died! You know what that means, right?" When it became obvious by the look on my face that I had no idea what he was talking about, Tim appeared dumbfounded. "Please tell me you are not totally dim."

Tim awaited my response, but all I could offer was raised eyebrows and a blank look.

"Come on! The song "American Pie" is about the death of Buddy Holly. Tell me you know that!" Tim demanded with passion in his voice. "Come on!"

"Really? I thought no one knew the meaning of "American Pie" but Don McLean."

"Yeah, I think that's true, but he sings about the plane crash. Remember? 'But February made me shiver, with every paper I'd deliver. Bad news on the doorstep.' Remember? He couldn't remember if he cried when he read about the widowed bride on the day the music died."

"Yeah, I remember that."

Tim stood up and looked at me. "Gary, he's singing about the news of the plane crash killing Buddy Holly, Ritchie Valens, and the Big Bopper! He's talking about Buddy Holly's young widow—the widowed bride. That's the infamous day the music died."

"His first name is Big and his last name is Bopper?" I asked.

"Stay with me. Focus. I am trying to teach you something," Tim responded. By now he was clearly frustrated.

"Okay, okay, I'm focused."

"You do know about "American Pie," right?" Tim asked.

"Yes, of course. I know the song but I had no idea who the widowed bride was." I paused and thought about it. "So the day the music died is the day these three guys were killed in the plane crash?"

Tim just shook his head in disbelief and let out a deep sigh. "Sometimes I worry about you," he answered, lowering his voice and his eyes as he tried to refocus on his work. A few seconds passed in silence and then Tim looked up at me again. "What planet are you from?"

"I really didn't know he was that popular," I said. Looking back now, that answer must have confirmed to Tim that I grew up on Mars. "Tim—I was born in July of 1954. You said he died in what, 1959? I was still four years old! How would I know Buddy Holly?"

"Okay, well, you are the only person on earth past puberty who doesn't know who Buddy Holly is—or was. Geez, Gary. The guy is a cultural icon for Pete's sake. He helped create a musical movement that changed a generation and the course of music forever."

"Really? Buddy Holly did that?"

Tim closed his eyes and shook his head. "I'm not talking to you for a while. I need to finish this memo and let your lack of pop cultural awareness sink in."

I am an anomaly and I know it. I grew up in a Rock & Roll music vacuum. At a very young age I joined a drum & bugle corps. My passion for rudimental drumming immersed me in marching music. During my teen years, drum & bugle corps played more jazz and classical pieces, so I became a fan of both genres. I loved Beethoven, Mozart, Bach, Stan Kenton, Buddy Rich, and Maynard Ferguson. I joined concert band and jazz band in junior high. We didn't play any rock music there.

My dad was of the WWII generation and he was not at all a fan of Rock & Roll or what he saw developing culturally in the 1960s. I largely ignored the music of that era. My dad was a Country & Western music fan, so Billy Grammer, Hank Williams, Ernest Tubb, Ray Price, and George Jones is what was played in our home.

I went on to earn a degree in music education. Playing Rock & Roll in my college would have been blasphemy during those years, so once again I paid little or no attention to the musical wave that was sweeping the country. I had a brief stint playing drums for the Country star Ray Price and the Cherokee Cowboys, but my exposure to Rock & Roll was nearly nonexistent. I get why I didn't know much about Buddy Holly, and I also realize I'm quite unusual for my generation.

I explained all this to Tim, who shook his head and sighed again. "Gary, you missed an entire decade of music."

He's right. I loved The Beatles song "Eleanor Rigby," but only because my drum & bugle corps, the Cavaliers, played it. And somehow I had it in my head that all rock & roll was created and spread from Liverpool, England . . . not Lubbock, Texas.

"Just when you think you know someone . . . ," my voice trailed off.

"What do you mean?" Tim asked.

"My mother-in-law. She is the sweetest human being I know. Almost like a Donna Reed or June Cleaver kind of woman. I've never heard her mention Buddy Holly or any other band. I've never known her to listen to music of any kind. I always figured her for a Benny Goodman-Tommy Dorsey type, not a rocker." I paused to think about Norma. "Next thing you know, she'll confess she was dropping acid with Jimmy Hendrix in the sixties."

"Please tell me you didn't just say that!" Tim exclaimed. "You missed that entire era and you don't even understand what you just said or who Jimmy Hendrix was!" Tim laughed. "Don't act like you do. My kids would say you're being a poser, so stop it." Tim turned back to his laptop. "Arlene's mom is hipper than you. That's too funny."

Tim's right. She is hipper than me.

I'm depressed.

Chapter 2

Look at me

The day arrived. We drove to Independence, Iowa under dark and overcast skies, the sun refusing to show itself the entire time. It was our typical Illinois to Iowa trip. Each time we approach the Iowa border I hold my nose and make pig sounds, just as I have done for thirty-five years. But once we are halfway across the Interstate 80 Bridge spanning the Mississippi River, Arlene breaks into a rousing version of the Iowa Corn Song, which invariably ends with her screaming "Iowa, Iowa, that's where the tall corn grows!"

Yes I understand how crazy this sounds, but this is the ritual we have repeated over and over for our entire marriage. Thirty miles across the border, as always, we exit the interstate and pull into the Iowa 80 Truck Stop, which bills itself as the world's largest. After walking through the ailes looking at their unusual wares, we climb back into the car for the final leg of the trip to Independence.

We arrived around 4:00 p.m. to find Norma and her husband Bob already dressed and pacing. After exchanging our usual greetings and hugs Arlene and I unpacked.

"Your mom is dressed and ready to go," I observed.

"She's really looking forward to this. This is important to her," Arlene replied while holding a pair of shoes in each hand. Her eyes darted back and forth as she wondered which to wear. "I think she's a little upset that we're late." Early in our marriage Arlene used to ask my advice about what to wear, but she learned quickly I'm not much help in the fashion department.

"We're not late, Arlene." I glanced at my watch. "The concert doesn't start for three and a half hours, and it's only a thirty-minute drive."

"I know, but she is so excited and I'm excited for her." Arlene held up the pair in her left hand. I nodded and she put them on the floor. "You're a musician. This should be fun. Please enjoy this tonight, for my mom."

I reached for Arlene and pulled her close. "Of course I will. I am going to The Winter Dance Party with the two most beautiful women in Iowa."

(I know how to get out of trouble.)

We left Independence an hour later and drove to Waterloo for dinner at Famous Dave's and then made the short drive to the Gallagher Bluedorn Performing Arts Center on the campus of the University of Northern Iowa in Cedar Falls. The people in these parts have always taken their arts very seriously. The facility is beautiful, but what was waiting for me in the lobby when we entered was not what I expected at all. I thought the place would be filled with a younger Rock & Roll crowd brimming with enthusiasm. Instead, I entered to discover that I was the youngster. I'm fifty-five.

When I spotted an event poster I walked over to take a look. Across the top it said "John Mueller's Winter Dance Party" and below were pictures of Buddy, Ritchie, and the Big Bopper. Arlene and her mom posed in front for a photo before walking away to mingle with others.

I was studying the poster when a woman about ten years my senior asked, "Aren't you excited? I can't believe this night is finally here. I've been looking forward to this for months!"

"This night?" I asked. I knew what she meant, but I really have no idea why I pretended I didn't.

"Tonight! The Winter Dance Party, of course! I've been counting the days. I was so afraid I was not going to get a ticket, but I'm here and it's like a dream!" The woman looked sixty-something but acted and sounded like a teenager. When I didn't respond with the same youthful enthusiasm, she repeated, "Aren't you excited?"

"Sure . . . well . . . yes . . . I guess." I offered a small shrug. "I'm here."

She laughed. "Not a fan of Buddy Holly or John Mueller's Winter Dance Party?"

"No, I'm not a fan. I'm here with my mother-in-law. We brought her for her birthday. I'm sure I'll find it interesting, though."

"For her birthday? That's nice. Your mother-in-law is a fan?"

"Yes, she is—and to my surprise. I had no idea."

"Wow," she replied, nodding and smiling. "Your mother-in-law is hipper than you!"

Hmm. Déja vu, I thought. I wondered if she knew Tim. "These pictures," I motioned toward the poster. "Are these the original performers or pictures of the impersonators?"

"Oh my," she placed her hand over her mouth and shook her head as if she could not believe I asked the question. "Get in the spirit! There are no impersonators here. We are at the Winter Dance Party! I'm here to see Buddy, Ritchie, and the Big Bopper. It's February 1959!" With that, she turned on her heel like a teenager spurned and walked away as if she was afraid I would spoil the magic of the evening.

I thought for a moment about clicking my iPhone and asking Scotty to beam me up. I felt stuck in some sort of time warp.

In her mind she may have understood the reality of time, but in her heart she was there to bring her memories to life. I felt bad. The last thing I wanted to do was dampen her spirit. I was about to walk after her when I spotted Norma and Arlene approaching. Am I killing the magic for my mother-in-law? I needed to get in sync with the spirit of the evening so I asked them to stand next to The Winter Dance Party poster and took a picture.

The doors opened at 7:10 p.m. We walked in and sat down in the twelfth row, slightly to the right of the stage. They were great seats, but something seemed wrong with the set-up. All I could see were the drums, guitars, a double (upright) bass and a few microphones. Where was all the equipment? I looked all over the stage for the massive racks and towers of speakers usually associated with Rock & Roll, but they were

Arlene Moore and her mom, Norma Wurster Wigant Jackson, in front of the Winter Dance Party poster in Cedar Falls, Iowa. *Author*

nowhere to be seen. So this is what a 1959 Rock & Roll stage looked like, I thought.

Norma leaned over and said, "They're performing tomorrow night too, and both nights are sold out!" I nodded in reply.

Frankly, the news surprised me. They could fill this theater twice for an event like this? Of course, I knew little about Holly and even less about John Mueller and what he had to offer.

I'm a people watcher. I sat in my seat and observed as many people as possible and realized everyone had one thing in common: they were all smiling and excited. Everyone looked and acted as if they were there for a very special reason, and that reason was in the building and at that moment just a few yards away backstage. I realized again I needed to get with it. The enthusiasm was contagious.

At 7:30 the light dimmed and a screen lowered on stage. A video presentation began, complete with music and a history of the original Winter Dance Party. I learned more about Buddy Holly during those few minutes than I had learned in a lifetime. All of it was interesting, but nothing about it really grabbed me.

When a picture of Holly sitting on a chest freezer tuning his guitar appeared Bob, Norma's husband, leaned over to me and said, "That's from the kitchen at the ballroom at Electric Park in Waterloo." When the presentation ended the backstage announcer welcomed us to the Winter Dance Party starring the Big Bopper, Ritchie Valens, and Buddy Holly. Several musicians walked out and the audience erupted with wild energy that grew even louder when the Big Bopper took the stage.

He was good, and to my surprise I recognized all of the music! I had no idea these were his songs. We learned that the performer was actually the son of the real Big Bopper. He explained that his mother was so hurt by the death of his father that she did not tell him much about his dad's life as a performer until 1989. That touched an emotional chord within me. I had not known my father had a fascinating life in baseball and World War II until the night before he died in 1983—a story I recounted in the book *Playing with the Enemy*. I suddenly felt a strange connection to what was happening on stage. The son of the Big Bopper, Jay Richardson, performed "White Lightning," "Big Bopper's Wedding," "Someone Watching Over You," and then, of course, "Chantilly Lace."

Next on stage was Ray Anthony as Ritchie Valens. When he appeared the eruption of enthusiastic applause surprised me. As the performer who played Ritchie began strumming his guitar and singing, I was struck by his level of talent. This was a high energy show performed with an impressive display of musicality. Ray, performing as Ritchie, played lots of songs, including "Come On Let's Go," "Framed," and "La Bamba," but "Donna" stole the show. As he was preparing to leave the stage I wondered how the Buddy Holly performer could possibly top all this. The Big Bopper and Ritchie Valens were really amazing.

John Mueller, the man who would be Buddy, walked onto the stage with confidence and projected instant charisma. The audience broke into wild cheers. I leaned over and yelled to Arlene, "He looks exactly like the pictures of Buddy Holly in the video presentation!" She only nodded in reply, too interested in what was happening on stage to pay much attention to me. While Mueller was playing I kept thinking again and again, "I did not know Buddy Holly wrote this." "I did not know Buddy Holly performed this." I knew each and every song, and for the entire performance John Mueller had me believing I was seeing the real Buddy Holly.

The show continued and the time flew by. I was surprised at how much I was really enjoying the evening. The show was coming to an end and I felt bad for dreading the event. I appreciated the level of professionalism I was seeing and hearing. It was good. No—it was excellent and more than worth the time, effort, and money. But I couldn't imagine wanting to do it again. I enjoyed the experience, but was not a skeptic-turned-fan. It was fun, but once was enough.

"I'm going to end tonight with an original song I wrote in 1999 as a tribute to Buddy Holly," announced Mueller. "I've written two new verses honoring Ritchie and the Big Bopper, too."

I groaned. I wished he hadn't said that. If anything could take this enthusiastic crowd out of the moment, it would be a song written in 1999 for an audience that was living Buddy Holly five decades earlier. And there was no way it could live up to the quality of the original music. What was this guy thinking? I was about to hear a song written by a celebrity impersonator after hearing an evening of outstanding original music by the legends themselves.

This is going to be a train wreck.

Mueller began playing his guitar and singing "Hey, Buddy," but then spoke the next three words: "Look at me." And I did. I was suddenly and abruptly awestruck. I don't know exactly how to explain what I was feeling. It was as if John Mueller was speaking directly to me. He then said, "Listen to me," and again, I did. I listened to every word and it impacted me on an emotional level I could never have predicted. His words were deeply moving, the melody was haunting, and I felt a connection to the man on stage that was both indescribable and unimaginable.

The rest of the audience was listening just as intently and, like me, seemed spellbound. I imagined they were still at the 1959 Winter Dance Party, but the haunting melody and words had taken me somewhere else entirely. I was not just inside John Mueller's head, but inside his heart. I

John Mueller's popular Winter Dance Party rocking the night away. Here, Jay Richardson as the Big Bopper (far left) and Ray Anthony as Ritchie Valens (far right) join John as Buddy Holly (center) on stage for a couple songs. *John Mueller*

was feeling his emotion and listening to the words he had penned about the man whose music he performed. He was speaking directly to Buddy and I felt as though I had been personally invited in by John Mueller to witness his melodic conversation with a ghost.

"Hey, Buddy . . . I'll see you . . . on down the line . . ." were the song's last words.

I felt the magic. I had tears in my eyes. So did John Mueller.

When the performance ended and the lights went up I quickly wiped my eyes to hide my emotions from Arlene and anyone else close enough to witness my tears.

How could I explain this?

"Are you okay?" she asked, looking at me as if she knew something profound had just happened, but didn't know what.

"Yes, it was a great show—don't you think?" was the best I could muster. My words stumbled over themselves as they escaped my lips.

Arlene put her hand on my arm, squeezed gently, and smiled. "Thank you for doing this."

"No, thank you," I replied. "Thank you to your mom."

As we walked out, I kept turning to look at the empty stage. It was almost like a magnet and I was made of iron. I didn't want to leave, and the feeling was almost physical.

What just happened to me?

Chapter 3

I'm just sitting here reminiscing

We walked out into the lobby and saw that a long line had formed at an autograph table. As I noted earlier, it was hard for me to leave the theater. I felt drawn to say something to Mueller, but had no idea what words would come out of my mouth. Anyone who knows me would never accuse me of being tongue-tied, but I had no idea what to say even though I wanted to say something!

Bob asked me to drive. Instead of getting in line to greet Mueller we loaded into their new ruby red Buick Le Sabre and headed for home. I was making the turn onto Highway 20 when Bob mentioned again the picture of Buddy tuning his guitar while sitting on the chest freezer. "That shot was taken in Waterloo, Gary, at Iowa's Electric Park Ballroom."

"What is Electric Park?" I asked.

"It's an old ballroom. It's at Electric Park, which is next to the Hippodrome. It's owned, I believe, by the Cattle Congress. Back in the day it was quite the place. There was an amusement park and, of course, the ballroom."

Is Electric Park still around?" I inquired.

"Oh yeah," replied Bob. "It's still there. They'll never tear it down. It's part of Waterloo history. Tommy Dorsey, Guy Lombardo, Conway Twitty and of course Buddy Holly and others, they all appeared there."

I was surprised how much he knew about the subject and of course, my mind wandered. Is the freezer he sat on still there? Is the stage he performed on still around? I thought about driving the 20 miles to Waterloo tomorrow to see. But to see what? A five-decade old freezer? An empty ballroom whose best days were decades in the past? And why would I even waste my time thinking about all this?

"Is the freezer still there?" I blurted out as if I had been drinking coffee all morning and was suffering from a caffeine rush. I felt stupid even before I had uttered the last syllable. "Is the original stage still there?" I quickly added, hoping he would ignore the question about the freezer.

"Oh, yeah. I think the stage is built in as part of the old place," replied Bob as if it was a question he was asked with some regularity. "I doubt if the freezer's around, though."

I bet he thinks I'm an idiot, I thought. Still, I could not stop asking questions. "Bob . . . did you ever see the real Buddy Holly?"

"No, but he played all around here. His last performance was at the Surf Ballroom."

"Where is the Surf?"

"Clear Lake."

"Iowa?"

"Yeah, Clear Lake, Iowa. Over near Mason City," replied Bob as he pointed over his left shoulder.

I have many Mason City connections. John Skipper, a well-known baseball author and veteran newspaperman from Mason City mentored me as I wrote my first book, and Jim Zach designed the jacket for that book because he designs jackets for the publisher. And speaking of the publisher, Theodore P. Savas, the managing director of Savas Beatie, was born and raised in Mason City (eight miles from where Buddy Holly's plane went down). I knew that Meredith Willson, who composed *The Music Man* and *The Unsinkable Molly Brown*, was also from Mason City.

"Mason City," I mumbled aloud.

"What about it?" asked Bob.

"I just remembered something. About fifteen years ago I was flying in a private plane with my friend Roberto Martinez. Roberto was a flight instructor at the Kankakee airport. We landed for fuel in Mason City. Roberto and I were standing next to the wing watching the lineman fuel the plane when Roberto mentioned to me that this was the airport Buddy Holly took off from right before his plane crashed. The lineman—he was probably no more than about eighteen—overheard our conversation and said, 'Yeah, and the wreckage from the plane is still in that hangar right over there,' pointing to a row of hangars."

Bob's eyebrows arched in surprise. "Was it?" he asked.

I shrugged in reply. "I have no idea if the kid was just showing off and making it up, or if the plane was still there, tucked away in some remote corner of the airport." I paused. "If you think about it, it sounds like one of those urban myths." But was it? Was I once that close to perhaps the most famous piece of aviation wreckage in American history?

"I guess the Clear Lake airport makes sense," offered Bob.

I shook my head. "Maybe it is, but I doubt it."

"Well, I guess it has to be somewhere," Bob continued.

Back then, I could not have cared less about Buddy Holly. If that kid had invited me to see the wreckage, I probably wouldn't have bothered. But after seeing John Mueller perform as Buddy Holly something had changed inside me. Now I needed to know.

"I'll find out," I said. "Is the Surf still there?"

"Oh yeah—it's a landmark. They'll never tear it down," Bob answered, emphasizing the word "never."

"How far is it from here?" I asked.

He thought for a moment. "I guess about two hours from Independence, give or take a few minutes."

"Really? It's that close?"

"Yeah, it's not far."

We pulled into the garage at Norma and Bob's home. They were exhausted and after telling us they had a wonderful time, went straight to bed. Arlene and I headed for our room, where I detoured to get my laptop.

"What are you going to do with that?" she asked.

"I have to Google something."

Arlene cast a suspicious glance in my direction and went into the bathroom to brush her teeth. I sat on the bed, brought up the search window, and hesitated. What should I search for? I thought a moment and typed the two obvious words: Buddy Holly.

To my complete surprise, 9,390,421 results shot back at me. Tim was right. The fact that I was in my fifties and knew next to nothing about Buddy Holly was weird. Millions of web references and I don't know more than his name? He's everywhere on the Internet and I was starving for any information I could find. I scanned the first page of listings and decided to begin with the Wikipedia listing. After devouring that I clicked on the official site. Then something about musical influences. Then . . . I was reading everything that seemed remotely interesting as fast as I could.

Wait! John Mueller must have a website, right? I easily found www.yourbuddyjohn.com and smiled at the cleverness of the name. At first I admit to feeling a bit let down. His website was nothing fancy. I guess I was expecting something super modern and high tech. Within a few seconds it was obvious there was more behind the design than functionality. If there had been an Internet in the late 1950s or early 1960s, this is what a website might have looked like back then. Near the bottom was an embedded video of his tribute song "Hey, Buddy." I clicked it and the song came to life for the second time that evening.

The first few notes from John's guitar were playing when Arlene walked into the room, toothbrush in hand. "What are you listening to?"

"Don't you recognize it?" I shot back excited. "This is the final song from tonight's performance!"

"Is it? Why are you listening to it again?" She stuck her toothbrush into her mouth and continued brushing.

"Don't you find yourself wanting to hear it again?"

"Not really," she slurred through a mouth full of toothpaste. "It isn't one of Holly's original songs." She walked back into the bathroom, rinsed the toothpaste from her mouth and leaned back into the bedroom. "Play 'Peggy Sue.'"

I ignored her request, my mind still firmly fixed on what I was convinced was a masterful piece of music. "Of course it's not a Holly original," I agreed, "but this song is so well written. It's really triggered something inside me."

"Triggered something? Oh boy," she said with a wide smile. "That'll be the day that you start obsessing over something."

"Very funny." I smiled back. Arlene knows me better than anyone, and when I latch onto something. . . . I clicked on the icon to start the song again, clicked the pause button, and looked up. "Come and sit next to me. I want you to listen to each and every word. You can also watch the video for the song. It's really well done."

Arlene sat on the side of the bed next to me, put her head on my shoulder, and stifled a yawn. "If I watch this, can we turn it off and go to bed afterward?"

"Yeah, in a bit. I have a couple of things I want to look up first." I clicked play and the video came to life.

"Hey, Buddy"

Tribute to Charles Hardin "Buddy" Holley
(Correct last name spelling)
by John Mueller

Hey, Buddy…**Look At Me**, I'm just sittin' here **Reminiscing**
And I know your **Words Of Love** will **Not Fade Away**…
But something's still missing.
Well, Alright but **It's So Easy** to feel this way,
I start **Wishing** you were here but I know **That'll Be The Day**
And **Maybe, Baby** I shouldn't be so sad
But it starts **Raining In My Heart** when I think of all you had…

Hey, Buddy . . . I got those **Early In The Morning** blues
But **I'm Gonna Set My Foot Right Down** on my **Valley Of Tears**,
I got nothing to lose.
I'm gonna start **Rocking Around With Ollie Vee**

Everyday a **Rock-a-Bye-Rock** will be the cure for me
I'm gonna tell my blues **Don't Come Back Knockin'**
Cause I'm **Changing All Those Changes** now and I'll be Rockin'…

Chorus:

Hey, Buddy…**Rave On** and sing us a song
Baby, Won't you Come Out Tonight
We're all **Looking For Someone To Love** down here
You help us make it thru these **Blue Days And Black Nights**

Hey, Buddy…**Listen To Me**, I got a **Girl On My Mind**
And when I play her your **True Love Ways**…
Oh, Boy, it works every time.
You see now, **Love's Made A Fool** of me before
But now **It Doesn't Matter Anymore**
Cause your songs **Tell Me How** and **What to Do**
Yeah, **I'm Learning The Game** now with **Peggy Sue**…

Repeat Chorus. Repeat Chorus again with new lyrics:

Hey, Buddy…**Rave On** your songs live on
Baby, Won't You Come Out Tonight
We've been **Crying, Waiting, & Hoping** for so long
Help us make it thru these **Blue Days And Black Nights**

Hey, Buddy . . . We'll see you on **Down The Line**.

Bold highlights denote titles of songs
written and/or performed by Buddy Holly

Words and Music by John Mueller
Copyright 1998 Mueltone Music ASCAP

When the song ended I looked over at Arlene. "Isn't it moving? I just love this song."

"I know. I can tell." Arlene leaned over and kissed my cheek. "Good night."

My laptop and I moved into the family room. I spent the next four hours listening to the song over and over and reading and watching everything on the Internet I could find about Buddy and John. I read the accident report and looked at the pictures from the crash site. I watched John Mueller clips and clips of others visiting the actual crash site. I looked at pictures of historical "Buddy locations" in Lubbock. The more I learned, the more I wanted to know. Hours slipped past.

It was early in the morning when I found myself clicking on the "contact John" button on Mueller's website to send an email to john@yourbuddyjohn.com.

But what should I write? I started and stopped several times, unsure of what to say or ask. The last thing I wanted to do was come across like some nut. I finally decided to send him a thank-you note to let him know how much I enjoyed the show and how much I loved "Hey, Buddy." I reread my brief email and hit send.

And then it hit me. I was 55 and had just written the first fan letter of my life. But who and what was I a fan of, exactly? Buddy Holly? John Mueller? A song? I wasn't really sure.

What I did know for certain was it was time to get some sleep.

*　　*　　*

The next morning Arlene and her mom were trying to decide whether to go into Waterloo to do some shopping. I surreptitiously opened the GPS on my iPhone, cast a quick glance at Arlene to see if she was paying attention to me, and typed in "Clear Lake, Iowa." It was 117 miles away. How much trouble would I be in if I was MIA for five or six hours? Could I make it there and back before anyone noticed I was missing? Sadly, I concluded I could not.

A few minutes later Arlene and Norma left to shop at Dillards at The Crossroads Mall in Waterloo. (Dillards is Arlene's favorite store and we don't have one near our home in Illinois. A trip to Iowa is not complete unless Arlene hits a Dillards.) With the two women gone and Bob taking a nap, I had the morning free! I headed over to the Independence Public Library in search of a place with a faster Internet connection and promptly found it.

Independence Public Library is a new facility and was lightly occupied on this Saturday. I found my way to a comfortable chair near an electrical outlet, plugged in my laptop, and got to work. The first place I visited was www.yourbuddyjohn.com to watch the "Hey, Buddy" video once more. I clicked back to YouTube and found recordings of pilgrimages of people from around the globe who visited the crash site and posted their videos online for the world to see. Why?

Why would they do that? Why travel to a remote cornfield in north-central Iowa, record the experience, and place it on the net? As proof they were there? Why was this so important to them? I watched and read everything I could find in a three hour period that felt more like three minutes.

During that time I pulled my yellow legal pad from my computer case and began a "to do" list.

- Download every song recorded by Buddy Holly available on iTunes. Listen and try to understand who he was.

- Visit Electric Park in Waterloo and see if the freezer still exists. (Why?)

- Visit Lubbock, Texas, and Buddy Holly's final resting place. (Why?)

- Rent and watch The Buddy Holly Story.

- Download "American Pie." (The song, not the movie).

- See what I can find out about Don McLean's interest in the day the music died.

- Contact John Skipper in Mason City and see what he knows.

- Visit the Surf Ballroom in Clear Lake and while there, the nearby crash site.

- Find out if the plane still exists and where? (Why?)

- Write about everything that moves me and try to figure out why.

- Call Jim Riordan. (If anyone knows Buddy Holly, it will be Jim)

- Call Tim Milner. (See if he plays Holly on his radio stations)

- Call John Mueller.

- Call Ted Savas. Ted's from Mason City. See what he knows.

- What else? What am I missing? Who am I missing? What should I know?

There was more. I was sure of it. After some items on my list I had placed a "why?" in parenthesis because I didn't understand "why" I wanted this task on my list. I guess I felt it should be there. No logic really, just pure feelings. There was more I would want to know, but I didn't know yet what it is I didn't know, so it was hard to know what I would need.

My ringing cell phone pulled me out of my "Holly" trance. A couple of patrons shot a "Don't you know better" glance in my direction. I cringed with embarrassment, mouthed the word "Sorry!" in their direction, leaned over in a vain effort to be discreet, and whispered "Hello?"

"Where are you? You aren't trudging around some cornfield near Mason City are you?" demanded Arlene.

"That's silly. Why would you ask that?" I tried to sound offended, but try pulling that one off while leaning into a library corner and whispering into a cell phone.

"Because I know you," she said. "I've seen you obsess this way before." There was a moment of silence on the phone. "You are, aren't you? I knew it!"

"Obsess? What are you talking about? Don't be silly." I said in my best non-defensive voice. "I'm at the Independence Library and I'll be home in ten minutes."

"The library? Okay, I'm timing you." I heard Arlene laughing as she hung up the phone. I packed my laptop and headed for the door.

"Mr. Moore?" I turned to see a librarian waving in my direction. "Can I bother you to sign this before you leave?" She held up a hardcover copy of *Playing with the Enemy*.

"Of course," I responded with a smile. "It would be my pleasure." As she handed me the book I asked, "What do you know about Buddy Holly?"

"Only the basics, I guess. He created a large volume of music in a very short time that has been recorded and re-recorded through all the years since his death. Why do you ask?"

"Just curious," I answered.

She smiled. "I bet you attended the Winter Dance Party last night in Cedar Falls, right?"

"I did! How'd you know?"

"There was a group of women in here this morning and it was all they could talk about. Most of them attended last night and a few tried to get tickets for tonight again but it is sold out," she said.

"Does this surprise you?"

"Does what surprise me?"

"That they were all hyped up about a guy who's been gone for over fifty years."

She furrowed her brow for a moment in thought. "Not really. It was an older group. It's their music. I'm sure it allows them to relive their past and remember their younger days." She paused. "No, it doesn't surprise me, but when I say it's their music, I don't mean it is not relevant or still current today. I guess I mean that back then, their age group was on the cutting edge of a new kind of music. We have our music today, good and bad, because of them."

"So you view it as 'their' music?" I really wanted to understand what she meant.

"No, I didn't mean it that way," she replied quickly. "They were his age back then. They were eyewitnesses to the musical movement. It was new and like I said, cutting edge. I love it. 'Peggy Sue' is one of my favorite songs. I guess I mean it is their music and we have inherited it. I don't know if I am making sense." She laughed.

"You are," I assured her. "Thank you. That was very insightful."

"I was just thinking," she continued. "Would you be willing to come back for a book signing and discussion?"

"Sure, I would love to do that." As anyone who knows me can tell you, getting me to shut up when I am passionate about something is darn near impossible. Any excuse to talk about my dad's unusual baseball career, the World War II generation, and baseball was fine with me. I handed her a card, thanked her, and headed for the door.

Before I had taken two steps the librarian blurted out, "You know he died here, right?"

I stopped and turned around. Her bright smile was gone, and in its place was a somber, heavy look. "Here?" I asked.

"In our state," she clarified, pointing west. "A farm near Mason City."

"Yes. I know." We looked at each other for a moment. She nodded and I turned for the door.

I walked to my car surprised that this thirty-something librarian in small Iowa town knew so much and had such an interesting opinion of early Rock & Roll. When I asked what she knew about Buddy Holly, I really expected a shrug and a response of "not much." I was also surprised she stopped me to say that he died here. She seemed sad. She hadn't been born yet.

I opened the door of my car and loaded my laptop case in the back seat. "Is Tim right?" I wondered. "Do I really know less about Buddy Holly than any other human being?" Maybe twenty-four hours ago that was true, but not today.

When I opened the door and walked into Norma's and Bob's home, Arlene and her mom looked at me and laughed. "What's so funny?" I asked.

Arlene got up from the table, walked to the door, and picked up my boots as I took them off. She examined the soles and laughed again. "No mud!" she proclaimed. I think she was disappointed.

"What?" I asked.

"I'm surprised." Arlene and her mom chuckled again. "I thought for sure you were out walking through a bean field somewhere looking for ghosts."

"That's silly. What would make you think that?"

"I know you, Gary. I know how you are when you get that look in your eyes. When your interest moves to intrigue . . . then obsession. I know what you do. I've seen it before."

I gave her the "Let's change the subject look" and she dropped it.

When I walked downstairs to put my laptop away I mumbled, "The ground is still frozen. There wouldn't be any mud." I would have gotten away with it. I should have gone.

My iPhone vibrated just as I hit the last step. I had an email. I looked at my phone and felt a quick wave of anxiety. It was from John@yourbuddyjohn.com.

> *Hello Gary, thanks for the nice response and interest. I have another show tonight and will be traveling all day Sunday. I will give you a call on Monday when not so chaotic.*
>
> *Cheers, John*

He answered. Now what?

Chapter 4

I know your words of love

My phone rang on Monday afternoon at 3:05 p.m. It was John Mueller. I tried not to let my enthusiasm make me sound like a fan. We exchanged pleasantries and I confessed my deep intererst with his song and his tribute to Buddy Holly. I told him I'd love to know more, but was not sure what there was to know. Fortunately, he did not treat me like I was a stalker. I was sure beginning to feel like one.

John was a real gentleman. I told him that I really didn't know enough about him or my recent fascination with him, the musician he portrayed, or their music together, but I had an urge to write about it. But write what? I wasn't sure. He seemed intrigued by my sudden and passionate interest.

I found him to be friendly and humble, but most importantly, not Buddy Holly. That was important to me. In the mid 1980s I met an Elvis impersonator who thought he was Elvis. Seriously. This guy believed he was Elvis Presley. It was weird. He never left character even off the stage. Compound that experience with the movie I've seen several times called Honeymoon in Vegas, starring Nicholas Cage. The entire backdrop of the movie is an Elvis impersonator convention, complete with the "Flying Elvis's" parachute team. Some impersonating Elvis were black, some were Chinese, some fat, some skinny. You get the picture. Let's just say I began this adventure with a bias against musical impersonators.

During our initial conversations John made it clear that he is an actor and a musician—and excellent at both—playing the role and music of Buddy Holly. I exhaled a sigh of relief that he was anchored in reality.

I also learned that John has had numerous roles on various stages, television shows, soaps, as well as an ongoing gig in a one-man show called The Wonder Bread Years. He has also recorded a couple of albums of his own music, which is quite unique and much different than Buddy Holly's songs. John Mueller is secure in his own identity. We discussed my deep interest in Holly—sudden and utterly unexpected, but that is how these things work with me—and my desire to explore further the possibility of writing about it. We ended our conversation by agreeing to speak again and see where it all goes. I sent him a copy of my first book so he could get a better understanding of my writing style.

What makes John Mueller tick? What made Buddy Holly tick? What was making me tick in this new and unexpected direction? I wasn't sure where my fascination lay and why. I just knew I couldn't get that song—or Buddy Holly—out of my head.

Chapter 5

Will not fade away

I wonder. What is it about a body of work that does not die with its creator? What makes art, art? And why do some creative works stand the test of time and others do not? When we happen across creative "genius" in any walk of life, why is it that we rarely recognize the brilliance operating right in front of our eyes until it is gone?

Fifty-plus years later, Buddy's music still stands the test of time, both in its original form and as recorded in diverse styles by numerous artists. Is it because of a tragic death at an age too young? Is it because Don McLean memorialized his life by way of a melodic riddle in a song? Or is it because the music that originated in the heart and head of a young man from Lubbock, Texas, was unique, creative, and touched the hearts of millions both then and now? Is it really that good? And if so, how did I miss it?

As my journey to discover Buddy Holly deepened, so too did my appreciation for his music. Much like the word "hero," people have thrown the word genius around so often that it has lost much of its meaning. I determined early in the writing process that I would not use "genius" in this book—but is it applicable in this case? Buddy's music is simple, but art is not solely judged or measured by its level of complexity. A case can be made that because his music is simple and still stands the test of longevity is a testament to his genius in and of itself. I'm at the very least open to the idea that maybe there is genius in his music. Millions of adoring fans certainly think so, and still proudly proclaim Buddy Holly was a musical genius. Who knows?

But of everything that I experienced from the stage on the night of the Winter Dance Party, it was the song "Hey, Buddy" and its creator and performer John Mueller that captured my interest. The song brought the event into perspective for me. It brought closure to the evening. It brought Buddy to my intense personal attention. Mueller's song about the man and legend he portrays squeezed an emotional trigger somewhere deep inside me that I did not know existed and still do not fully understand.

Mueller's song says many things on a number of levels. If you only scratch the surface, Mueller is simply paying tribute to Holly in a respectful and loving way. The song acknowledges that he is not trying to be Holly, and is simply working to keep Holly's music and story alive and in our collective consciousness:

"I know your words of love will not fade away, but something's still missing."

Of course that missing something is Holly himself. Mueller is right. Holly's words and music show no signs of fading away.

I think "Hey, Buddy" also demonstrates how much Mueller enjoys playing Holly's music, not only for his aging fans but for others (like me) who have never really heard him before or paid much attention to his music. I'm a perfect example of how Mueller's performance turned me into a Holly fan. Does Mueller have this effect on others? Since his performance I have bought a copy of every song I can find that Holly ever recorded, and have also purchased all of Mueller's songs.

"Hey, Buddy" clearly demonstrates the deep respect John Mueller has for the legend he portrays. Mueller's own talent as a songwriter and performer comes across with the message, "I don't need to be Buddy. I'm doing this out of love and respect for the artist I admire and have grown to know well." Mueller's talent stands on its own as a singer-songwriter and performer.

I can get to know Buddy through his music and by reading about him and his life. I am sure if I dig deep enough I could probably find friends, family members, and fans that saw him perform live. But I also need to get to know Mueller so I can better understand his words and music.

Maybe then I can get a grip on what is happening to me.

Chapter 6

But something's still missing

As I quickly learned, Buddy Holly was only really in the public eye for about eighteen months. There is enough information on Buddy just on the Internet to keep one reading for a lifetime. But what about John Mueller? After all, it was John who really introduced me to Buddy and sent me on this road in pursuit of him and his influence. So . . . who is John Mueller?

John was born in Wichita, Kansas, a dry and windy city similar to Lubbock, Texas but, as John is fond of saying, "Without the twang." He came along later in his parents' lives so his siblings were nine to eleven years older than him. There was a benefit to the age difference. "I got to listen to their record collections—Little Richard, Chuck Berry, Elvis, Jerry Lee Lewis, The Beatles," explained John. "And of course, Buddy Holly. It was a great musical education and one that stuck with me forever."

"While my friends in high school were listening to Blue Oyster Cult, Boston, and Van Halen, I was still groovin' on the great original beat of Rock & Roll. My entire family played musical instruments," he recalled. "I banged on a cigar box strung with rubber bands as a toddler. Eventually I graduated to a real guitar and was largely self-taught. The first song I remember being able to play from beginning to end was 'Peggy Sue.'"

John loved Buddy's music, but he also liked the fact that Buddy wore glasses and was not the perfect face, like Elvis. He was the kind of Rock & Roll star that a kid from Kansas could try and emulate. Buddy wrote and produced his own songs and John loved Buddy's independence.

Life in Kansas was good for John. He grew up playing baseball, hot rodding in his Chevy Malibu, and working at drive-in theaters where he was bitten by the acting and entertainment bug.

"I worked concessions and would watch the same movie every night memorizing each actor's lines," John recalled.

And so John, like thousands of kids before and after him, headed out to the left coast with his sights set on the silver screen.

"I was in Hollywood," John began. "I answered an audition call for a show called 'Be Bop A Lula,' which was kind of an avant-garde play about Gene Vincent and Eddie Cochran holed up in an English hotel room. Buddy came to them in a nightmare sequence. I had to sing, act, and play like Buddy yet with a devilish twist. Somewhat bizarrely, the play was produced by Adam Ant and John Densmoore of The Doors. I got cast on the spot—a rarity for me!"

John continued: "A few years later the American Heartland Theatre, owned by Hallmark Cards in Kansas City, Missouri, produced the first regional production of 'Buddy: The Buddy Holly Story,' and I got cast in it as Buddy. This was a life changing experience as the show was so well received that it led to other productions for me in Chicago, San Diego, Toronto, and Miami. It was amazing for me to experience what Buddy must have felt with the audience reactions. It was also the first time I was able to combine my acting training and singing/guitar skills together. It gave me immense confidence in front of an audience and was invaluable."

As John spoke, I wondered at what point he realized that he and Buddy would become inseparable.

"Then, in 1999, before the 40th anniversary of the Winter Dance Party tour, Dennis Farland called. He had seen me in the Kansas City production of 'Buddy' and wanted to know if I was interested in doing some sort of a 40th anniversary trailing of the original tour," explained John. "He wanted me to drive to all the existing venues and show slides of historic photos, talk to audiences, and perform with karaoke tracks of the old songs."

John had a larger, more expansive, vision of the possibilities. "I took it a big step farther and replied, 'Let's do something never before attempted: Let's do what they did! An actual concert on the same dates at the same venues with a real band and performers!'"

Dennis thought about it and may have even thought John was a little nuts. Over the course of several conversations, however, it all came together. "I found a sound guy out of Wichita who was game—Jeff 'The Iron Man' Priddle," explained John. "He unloaded tons of sound equipment and our backline (amps, drums, etc.) every night after driving eight or nine hours! Did I mention he did this by himself? We drove ourselves in a fifteen-passenger van and realized firsthand how tired the originals must have been and why Buddy would have wanted to charter a plane."

As John explained it to me, including Clear Lake, Iowa—which was not intended to be the last stop—the 1959 Winter Dance Party was eleven shows in a row with no days off, and included horrendous winter travel weather and very poor routing by the GAC organizers. "They were in New York City and apparently did not have access to a map," was how John put it.

"Like Buddy, we ended at the Surf Ballroom on February 2, 1999, forty years later to the day," he said. "I was so exhausted I'd lost my voice. Everyone in our little entourage was pulling double duty: hotels, marketing, driving, and hard, hard work. We had no idea who would even show up. But it was immensely successful and ever since then the fans have been asking us to come back every year."

One of the aspects of John's career I found interesting was his relationship with Buddy's family and friends and of course, Buddy's wife Maria Elena Holly. The world became acutely aware of Maria Elena through Don McLean's song "American Pie," where he forever immortalized her as the "widowed bride." Maria Elena has a reputation as a resolute protector of the Buddy Holly legacy. She has been known to shut down impersonators if she didn't feel they were a good representation of the Buddy Holly brand. Maria Elena says John is different than all the rest and is the only person she endorses. Coming from the wife of Buddy Holly, that's a huge stamp of approval.

I asked John about his relationship with Maria Elena: "When did it all begin?"

"My relationship with Maria Elena started in 1999 when she found out through the grapevine about our planned tour," John began. "She was not pleased initially and had no idea who I was. I think I sent her my publicity shot—the one still used today which and has been used mistakenly as a real photo of Buddy on countless European CD collections of Buddy's music. I also sent her reviews from the Kansas City, San Diego, and Chicago productions of "The Buddy Holly Story." I think I also sent a CD of me singing his songs. Former Cricket member Niki Sullivan, who through the years has become a good friend and supporter, may have even placed a call to her, or she found out he approved of my portrayal. I really don't remember now."

John paused to think a moment before continuing. "At any rate, Maria came around, but the best thing occurred when I asked her to actually join us on tour one year. I didn't really think she would. To my surprise, she did! Maria saw the show, danced on stage with us, and told me I had two left feet just like Buddy! We've had our disagreements over the years but nothing that has got in the way of our mutual respect and friendship. I've been grateful for her endorsement and support as she can be very protective of Buddy's image and who may be trying to benefit from it. I have great respect for her efforts. I've always tried to present Buddy's music in an authentic and sincere fashion without hyperbole. Perhaps that has kept me in good stead with her."

While talking with John it occurred to me that he has portrayed Buddy much longer than Buddy was in the public eye, and has performed the songs hundreds of times more than Buddy. "That's the biggest thing of all, isn't it?" John replied when I mentioned these observations to him. "I've reaped bigger rewards and have performed in front of more people than Buddy ever did, unfortunately. It's a somewhat guilty feeling, like something that I don't deserve." John thought for a moment before adding, "He deserved to know how much of an impact he made."

"And is still making. I'm evidence of that," I interjected.

"Exactly! Buddy deserves to know that people from all over the world still clamor for his music fifty years after he left us. He deserves to know that he would have had countless honorariums dedicated to him. Some entity would have done for him what they did for Roy Orbison later in his life, resurrecting his career with the Traveling Wilburys. Buddy would have had a night at the Lincoln Center with the President of the United States giving him a lifetime achievement award. Staggering to think of the endless awards and recognition he would have enjoyed." John paused. "Sadly, it was not meant to be. My only good feeling about this is that perhaps somehow my show is helping to honor and represent Buddy to keep him and his music alive."

John could never have predicted that his suggestion to Dennis twelve years ago would trigger a new career that is so successful he is in bigger demand today than ever before. "John Mueller's Winter Dance Party" tours and performs all over the nation and around the world with Ray Anthony as Ritchie Valens and Jay Richardson as J.P. "Big Bopper" Richardson. It is a testament to the music and the talent of Buddy, Ritchie, and the Big Bopper—but also to John and his tour. It's hard for me to understand how the originals could have been much better. Buddy's own friends and family marvel at how much John looks, performs, and sounds like Buddy.

Is John's work as Buddy Holly nothing more than an imitation of the original, or does it serve some higher purpose? In my case he introduced me to Buddy and he is keeping the flame alive and introducing the music to a whole new audience.

I needed to know more.

I need to see John perform again.

Chapter 7

Well alright

We all have unique characters in our lives. Jim Riordan is one of mine. Jim is an accomplished *New York Times* best-selling author who has written more than twenty books. *Break on Through*, a biography of Rock megastar Jim Morrison, is recognized as one of the best Rock & Roll biographies of all time. I have great admiration for Jim and when I see him, I still have those moments of awe as if brushing up against greatness. I have known Jim for a long time and know him to be a normal guy, though with a "different" view of life than most people I know. He's truly a breath of fresh air and he never fails to make me laugh.

Jim is much more than an author of note. He is still at heart a 1960s hippie. In some ways Jim is still raging against "The Man" and the "blood-sucking corporations" trying to turn us into money-spending purchasing zombies whose only purpose is to pad the pockets of fat white men smoking cigars and looking down on us little people from exquisite cherry inlaid boardrooms atop ivory towers in the world's financial centers. He still warns of the military-industrial complex that loves war as a consumer of military hardware that must be repurchased from them at a profit. In his mind the 1960s may not have been the wonderful idyllic love-making time he vividly recounts, but in his heart Jim is forever at Woodstock, even though he was not actually there to begin with.

Jim "Levi Storm" Riordan standing in front of a building he was trying to secure to start a local teen center. *Jim Riordan*

When John Mueller's song cast me off on this journey, one of my first thoughts was to call the only Rock oracle I know: Jim Riordan. But I couldn't find his phone number saved on my iPhone. Strange . . . I was certain it there before. . . .

After a minute or so of searching I recalled that I had stored Jim's number under the name Levi Storm—his alter ego. I touched my way down to the S listings and pressed call.

"Hello?"

"Levi Storm!" I yelled into the phone. It always makes Jim laugh.

"What kind of trouble are you causing today?" Jim asked.

"You know me, the garden variety, but that's not why I'm calling," I responded with my normal Gary enthusiasm. "I need to touch base with the only guy I know who may have the answers to my questions."

"Speak to me. Ask the secrets of life and I will share all that is, but only what I sense you are ready to hear." Seriously, that was Jim's reply. That IS Jim. You could hear the big smile in his voice.

"What can you tell me about Buddy Holly?"

Silence.

Jim knows me, and at that moment he was surprised I even knew the name. His mind was probably tossing around the concept that this was the first time in my life that the words "Buddy" and "Holly" ever came out of my mouth in the same sentence, let alone back-to-back.

"Jim?"

"Yeah, I'm here for you. Buddy Holly? He was a pioneer and ahead of his time in so many ways."

Another long pause.

I was certain he was ready to impart the meaning of Buddy's life and his purpose in the larger galaxy. I eagerly awaited the knowledge and wisdom of the man whom I believed knew—and had lived—everything about music. I heard the Great One draw a long breath and then continue.

"I don't know, man. He was a little before my time. Why do you ask?"

That was it? I felt as though all the air had been let out of my balloon. "Really? You don't know more about Buddy Holly?"

"I know the Stones had a hit early in their career that was a Holly cover—'Not Fade Away.'"

"The Stones?" I questioned.

"Sorry. I forgot who I was talking to," laughed Jim. "That would be the Rolling Stones. You know. A British Rock group that was an early part of the British invasion in the sixties." Jim paused for my reply. When I didn't respond he added, "'I Can't Get No Satisfaction'? Remember?" I was beginning to hear a tad of irritation and disbelief in his voice.

Wherever Tim Duggan was at that moment, I'm sure he was sensing what was going on and shaking his head in utter disbelief.

"Of course I know the Rolling Stones," I responded confidently. "The skinny guy with the big lips."

Jim chuckled. "Yeah. That guy. What's going on, man? Why the interest in Holly all of a sudden? What's shaking?"

"I'm not sure I can explain it, really," I began. "My mother-in-law is a fan. Arlene and I took her to a reenactment of the Winter Dance Party in Cedar Falls, Iowa, and something triggered this strange yearning to learn more. Not only about Buddy Holly, but also John Mueller and the impact they are both having—on me and millions of other people."

"Who's Mueller?" Jim asked. "I don't recognize the name."

"John Mueller is an actor and musician. He portrays Buddy Holly in this traveling reenactment of The Winter Dance Party. You know, the final tour for Holly, Valens, and the Big Bopper?"

"Sure, okay," Jim replied. "I'm with you."

"John is good. Really good. I never saw Holly so I have nothing to compare him to, but Mueller is really more than a musician-actor portraying Buddy Holly. He's written a song about Buddy that is so beautiful and so deep and moving on so many levels. The song has impacted me in a way I cannot explain. I'll send you the link."

"Great. I'll take a listen. But why this new found enthusiasm for Holly and Mueller?" Jim asked.

Let me be honest about something. I always feel insecure about my writing when I talk to Jim. He's the real deal, a very accomplished author with a long and successful track record. I hesitated before answering him. "I think I'm going to write about it." I said it as if Jim might laugh at my reason. He never does.

"Write about Buddy Holly? Really?" Jim was genuinely surprised. So was I. "I know The Beatles were big into Buddy. He was a big influence on McCartney," Jim continued. "I know Gary Busey. Did you know he was my neighbor in Malibu? Busey was nominated for an Oscar for his role in The Buddy Holly Story." Jim paused again. "You're going to write this?"

Jim's question made my insecurities rush in. "Not a biography," I blurted as if I was apologizing for something. "Nothing like your Morrison book, but about my new and strange obsession and the journey I'm on to learn more. More about Buddy Holly, about John Mueller, and about all the music I've missed. I just feel driven to do this. I can't really explain it better than that."

"Cool, man." Jim said.

I love it when Jim talks this way. Someday I'd love to respond to someone with that phrase, but it would sound stupid coming out of my mouth.

"Anything I can do to help?" I know Jim. When he asks, he means it.

"I'm certain there will be. Right now I don't even know what I don't know, so I have no idea what to ask."

"Cool."

I smiled. I wanted to say "cool" back, but my mouth would not cooperate. My subconscious screamed, "DO NOT SAY IT! IT WILL NOT BE COOL!" I know they (my mouth and subconscious) are right.

I began this conversation with the one and only Levi Storm with the full expectation that he not only knew everything about Buddy, but might even begin channeling the spirit of Buddy out of his mouth and into my ear. I was certain there was more and that Jim/Levi knew what others did not. But on that day, the magical and mystical Levi Storm was not pouring forth the answers I sought. Or maybe, just maybe, in his wisdom he knew I was not yet ready, not worthy to hear the truth. Yeah. I'd go with that rationalization. I wasn't ready to accept that Levi was stumped. He was just holding back until my heart and mind were ready.

"Cool, man," I whispered, more to myself than for Jim's benefit.

Jim laughed. "What'd you say?"

"Pool man," I responded. "Arlene wants me to call him today."

"Cool. Okay. Let me know if I can help. That it?"

"That's it."

Jim hung up his phone.

"Levi Storm has left the building!" I announced as I clicked off my iPhone.

Chapter 8

It's so easy to feel this way

Since Jim was unable to provide meaningful insight into Buddy's life and work, I began the search to learn more about Buddy on my own. Buddy was from Texas. That alone speaks volumes about him.

Texans are different than the rest of us. They are a rare breed of human beings. Texas is the only state that was once its own republic, and many there still believe it is (or wish it were so). The state's nickname is the "Lone Star" state. It's common to see flagpoles flying the Texas state flag with no American flag in sight. I have spent a lot of time on the road all across this great country of mine, and I have never seen this in any other state. It's not that Texans do not consider themselves Americans. They most certainly do. In fact, I believe Texans are in general a bit more patriotic than most. But they take the issue of their state independence quite seriously. As far as they are concerned, Texas voluntarily joined with the other states for reasons of security, commerce, defense, and convenience. They are proud to be Americans—but they are rabidly ecstatic about being Texans.

Did you know you can buy just about anything in the shape of Texas? Potholders, cookie cutters, cake pans, coasters, candles, you name it. If it's a household decoration or tool, you can find it in the shape of Texas. I think that's one reason the shape of Texas is the most recognizable shape of any state. Could someone on the streets of New York City correctly identify the shape of Indiana if you held up a cut-out of the state? How about Iowa? Arkansas? They won't have a clue. Show them the shape of Texas and they will know immediately.

It's the same with flags. Somewhere in almost every Texas home you will find a Texas flag or a picture of a Texas flag. Everyone knows the Texas flag by sight, but the average Illinoisan cannot describe their state's flag or recognize it if you show it to them. I love my state of Illinois, but this is true and I admit it. Here's the bottom line: we are Americans who live in Illinois; they are Texans who live in America.

To say Texans are proud people would be a comical understatement, sort of like saying there are lots of stars in the sky, or there is a lot of water in the ocean. The average individual Texan carries in his heart more state pride than all the people of Illinois combined carry for theirs. There are some states that run a distant second. Virginians, Tennesseans, and maybe those from Massachusetts carry their state heritage with high regard. Texans are simply a different breed. "Texas. A whole 'nother' Country" is their slogan. They say things like, "American by birth, Texan by the grace of God." And they believe it.

Texans believe that there are only two types of people on the planet: (A) Those who are from Texas, and (B) Those who wish they were. I'll make my confession here and now. I am solidly in the B group. I love Texas and I respect Texans. I am an Illinois boy, but you never catch me out of my boots. Most Americans refer to them as "cowboy boots," but to a Texan they are simply "boots."

Yes, I am a Texas wannabe. I get tears in my eyes when I stand in front of the Alamo. I get chills when I see the Longhorn marching band parading down the street. I get goose bumps when I see the Texas flag flying alone in a Texas breeze under the bright Texas sun with a Texas blue sky as the backdrop. I believe the sun is brighter there, the sky is bluer there, and of course, everything is bigger in Texas.

Let me sum all this up with the words of a San Antonio carriage driver. Arlene and I were in San Antonio for Fiesta. Fiesta is their celebration of winning their independence from Mexico. It's a two-week party and it's an absolute blast. We took a late night open air carriage ride through the city. As we passed in front of the Alamo, unprompted and for no apparent reason other than the pride of being a Texan, the carriage driver turned to us and said, "God is from Texas." He spit his tobacco off to the side and added, "That's why He is so great." For a moment I believed him. The carriage driver slowly turned back to the front and never said another word the rest of the ride. He didn't have to. He'd already said it all.

When I learned Buddy was from Texas I understood immediately the simple basics of his upbringing. I admit there are no absolutes in the world, but it's so very rare to find a Texan who is not glowing with Texas pride. This is especially true in the West Texas town of Lubbock. I believe Texas molds and forms its young children in ways other states and regions do not. I think it would be hard for Buddy to be from Texas and to have not been influenced in this manner.

A handgun was found at the airplane crash site outside Clear Lake, Iowa, in 1959 that was later identified as Buddy's. It caused quite a stir and several silly rumors. It made sense to me right away—of course Buddy had a gun. He was a Texan. It would have been unusual for him not to have a gun! I realize that is a stereotype, but still . . . how could anyone have been surprised? I thought again about the picture of Buddy in sunglasses tuning his guitar at Waterloo's Electric Park. Buddy was a quintessential Texan.

Texans are big on the Golden Rule and Buddy embodied it. "He truly treated everyone with respect," his friends are found of saying. "While recording, if someone made a mistake, Buddy would stop, laugh and say, 'We'll have to do that over again!'"

Friends are also the first to point out that the depiction of Buddy in the movie The Buddy Holly Story was not accurate at all. Actor Gary Busey did an amazing job in his portrayal of Buddy, but he didn't write the script. The movie Buddy was temperamental and at times sullen and withdrawn, while the real Buddy—as testified to by those who knew him best—was outgoing, and always had a smile on his face and a kind word to say about others.

The movie depicts Buddy as being from Texas but happy to move to and be in New York. The reality is that Buddy intended to return to Texas and build his recording studio in Lubbock, not the Big Apple. Texas roots run deep. You can take a Texan out of Texas, but he usually wants to return. Yes, I think to understand Buddy you need to start with an understanding of Texans.

I've heard Lubbock referred to as the "Buckle of the Bible Belt." Non-believers would call it an offhanded insult, while Bible-reading Christians would call it a compliment and a true statement. The Holley (correct family spelling) family would be in the latter group. Buddy was raised as a Baptist in a home where the Bible was a workbook, not a table decoration. It was used, not just admired. Gary and Ramona Tollett, back-up vocalists on "That'll Be the Day" and other Holly songs say that Buddy carried his Christianity into his adult life, and although he was not vocal about his beliefs, he was firm in his faith.

Buddy may not have worn his faith on his sleeve, but he sure lived it. As Saint Francis of Assisi put it, "Preach the Gospel at all times and when necessary use words." That was Buddy. He tithed (gave 10% of his earnings to his church) and his treatment of others was a reflection of his quiet but deep faith. I believe his family, his church, and his state were the strongest forces in creating the Buddy Holly his friends and fans loved so much.

Buddy was born at home on Labor Day, September 7, 1936. His full name is Charles Hardin Holley. Holley is the correct spelling of his name, but he adopted Holly because of a mistake on a recording contract. Almost immediately his parents, Lawrence Odell and Ella Pauline (Drake) Holley, began calling him "Buddy" because they thought Charles Hardin was such a big name for such a little boy.

Buddy was the youngest of the Holley children. He had two older brothers, Larry and Travis, and an older sister named Patricia. The home in which Buddy was born is now a Walmart parking lot. He was raised in a typical Texas middle class family. He attended Lubbock public schools. There was nothing unusual or unique about his upbringing to which we can point and say, "This event or incident created the Buddy we know and love." His life was shaped over twenty-two years by his faith, family, friends, and of course, his state.

I was struck most by the evolving realization that I would have really liked Buddy. He was a good person, always a kind word for others and the attention and success he enjoyed at a young age never took over his personality. He remained Buddy from Lubbock—a nice guy ready to take on the world and Rock the music and entertainment industries.

I have been blessed in my life to meet many famous people, including presidents, movie stars, and politicians. And I am almost always disappointed because I hoped for more but got less than I expected. When it comes to Buddy, the more I learned the more I liked him. In fact, I "liked" him a lot, but I really needed to find and talk to people who knew him, worked with him, and can give me firsthand information about the man and the legend.

Chapter 9

I start wishing you were here but I know that'll be the day

"We were sitting in a hotel restaurant in Clovis, New Mexico," Ramona reminisced over the phone with me. "Through the years, we have seen many Buddy Holly impersonators. Some do a pretty good job but nothing comes close to the original. Buddy was one of a kind," she paused. "I thought it would be impossible to accurately portray Buddy, but as we were sitting there, waiting to meet another who would try, I looked up from the table and out of the restaurant into the hotel lobby and almost dropped my coffee cup! I turned to my husband and said, 'Gary, look . . . its Buddy!' I literally lost my breath."

I was speaking on the phone to Gary and Ramona Tollett in Arizona from my home in Bourbonnais, Illinois. Their voices carried a sense of enthusiasm for the subject but also reflected their age. They were dear friends of Buddy, so I'm guessing they are in their seventies. Ramona and Gary knew Buddy Holly well. They were back-up singers for "That'll Be the Day" and "Looking for Someone to Love."

"We recorded with Buddy for no pay. He was a friend and we just wanted to help out," explained Gary. "That's what good friends do."

Buddy worked with Gary and produced several songs for his solo career. Buddy Holly and The Crickets backed Gary musically on his recordings of "Gone," "Go Boy Go," "Golden Rocket," and several others. "Buddy and the band backed me in the same way," Gary told me with real pride. "There was no money involved. We were all good friends and helped each other out when we could."

Gary and Ramona performed live with Buddy, traveled with him, broke bread and laughed with him. They were not just friends. They were good friends. Dear friends. Ramona steered our conversation back to her original meeting with John Mueller. "We were in Clovis [New Mexico] to meet John. He had made quite an impression traveling around the country portraying Buddy, and so when we were in Clovis where he was performing, he called and invited us to the hotel for breakfast. We really were not prepared for who arrived. John walked in without shoes and wearing worn blue jeans and a white T-shirt." Ramona laughed.

"Why is that funny?" I asked.

"That is what Buddy was wearing the last time we saw him," replied Ramona. She paused a few moments. It was easy to sense the emotions building inside her. "John could not have known it, but the coincidence

Gary and Ramona Tollett, who recorded and sang with Buddy Holly, standing in front of their home in Arizona.

Gary and Ramona Tollett

was quite moving. We made our introductions and sat down together at the table and the more we talked, the more we felt like we were seeing a long-lost friend."

Gary agreed. "We loved Buddy. He was a good man and we could never detect that the success had changed him one bit. He was kind, humble, and excessively polite. That was just the way he was raised. He was taught to be a gentleman from his earliest years. His faith and his family," he continued, "gave him a solid foundation to build a successful life and career."

There was no doubt about it. They truly loved Buddy.

"As we spoke casually, getting to know John Mueller, we found so many similarities. The warmth and humility of Buddy was also present with John. But there was more," Ramona continued. "The bone structure of his face, his smile—it was uncanny the similarities."

"John was my introduction to Buddy. His song, 'Hey, Buddy' set me on this path searching for more," I interjected. Both said they understood and that it was no surprise to them at all.

"As we expected, John asked us about Buddy," said Gary. "We told John as we tell everyone: Buddy Holly was a good and honest Christian gentleman. He never angered, never swore, and never had a cross word for anyone. Off stage he was shy and reserved. On stage, he came alive as if he owned the stage and was born to perform."

"He really did come alive on stage, didn't he?" I asked.

"Yes," Gary continued. "On stage he bubbled over with personality. We were performing together in Dumas, Texas, and Buddy was wearing a cotton sports coat. He was quiet and reserved as he prepared to walk out on the stage, but the moment he walked out he erupted with enthusiasm and brought the audience with him. Forty-five minutes later, he walked off stage and we could have wrung buckets of sweat out of that coat."

It was at this point in our conversation that Gary and Ramona shared a fascinating story with me. "Paul McCartney invited us to New York in 1999 for Buddy's birthday," began Gary. "Paul told us that Buddy was a tremendous influence on The Beatles, their beginning and early success. He said that they watched their recording of "That'll Be The Day" spin round and round. They listened to every word. Every note. They

John Mueller singing with former Buddy Holly friends Gary and Ramona Tollett. *John Mueller*

dissected it, trying to understand exactly what was being done musically. Every chord . . . every rhythm. They tried to figure out how to recreate Buddy's unique sound," Gary explained. "Then Paul looked at Ramona and said, 'We thought you were a bunch of black guys.' Of course, we laughed at that and Ramona stated the obvious, 'I'm not a black guy!' 'No, you are not. You're not even a black girl, I suppose,' Paul McCartney answered to more laughter."

"Paul has deep respect for Buddy Holly and the Crickets" Gary added. "You could tell in the way he spoke of Buddy. There was and still is a sincere and lasting reverence there."

I was really pleased to get to know Gary and Ramona and learn of their deep respect and friendship with Buddy. Throughout my conversation I kept telling myself I would not ask the question I am sure they are asked all the time . . . and then I asked it anyway. "Do you remember where you were when you heard the news of Buddy's death?" For a few seconds an uncomfortable silence passed between us. I was really wishing I had not asked when Gary answered.

"Yes, of course." His voice had changed. It was softer, laden with emotion.

"That was a sad, sad day," added Ramona.

Gary continued. "I was a student at Texas Tech in Lubbock at that time. I was driving to class when I heard the radio report. I could not believe what I was hearing. I immediately drove to the Physics Department to try and see Ramona before she found out."

"I was working at the Physics Department," Ramona interjected.

"Ramona was putting me through school. I arrived at her building and fortunately she had not heard about it yet."

There was a long pause. I wasn't sure how to restart the conversation, but Ramona began again and saved me from saying something embarrassing.

"We attended the funeral service at the church," she continued. "We just could not believe it. He was only twenty-two and at the top of his career. You are not supposed to die at twenty-two. He had so much going for him. His career. His new wife. She was pregnant, we learned later."

"Yes. I heard," I answered softly. "I've read that."

"The church was packed. Everyone loved Buddy," Gary said. "We did not go to the cemetery and have still not been there to this day."

That revelation surprised me. "Why didn't you go?" I asked, already suspecting the answer.

"I guess we just want to remember him as he was. It's only his body there anyway. Buddy is somewhere else," explained Gary. "We know where he is."

My questions were forcing them to relive the entire heartbreaking experience. Earlier I could hear the happiness in their voices as we spoke of their time and experiences with Buddy. But now all I could sense and hear was a palpable sadness as they spoke about the loss of their friend. It was clear, however, that Gary and Ramona found solace in their faith.

"You want to really know who Buddy Holly was?" asked Ramona.

"Yes, of course," I answered. Lately it was all I wanted to know.

"He bought his church new pews with his first royalty check." She paused to let that sink in before continuing. "That . . . was Buddy Holly."

The phone went silent.

Chapter 10

Maybe baby
I shouldn't be so sad

I was sitting in the Batavia (Illinois) Public Library in a make-shift green room (a children's story room that is not green) waiting to speak to a group of 150 local residents about my book *Playing with the Enemy*. They had selected my earlier effort for their "One Book, One Batavia" community-wide annual reading program. I was surrounded by the literary likes of *The Cat in the Hat*, *Curious George*, and *A Boy Named Pierre*, but my thoughts were not on the upcoming talk but rather on Buddy and his far-reaching impact. My conversation with Gary and Ramona was still weighing heavily on my mind and my heart.

The day before while I was touring the library, a charming young library executive named Stacey Cisneros, the Head of Adult Services, mentioned she was from Shell Rock, Iowa.

"Shell Rock? My wife Arlene is from Waterloo," I replied.

"Shell Rock is only twenty miles from Waterloo and my dad is originally from Waterloo," Stacey said enthusiastically. "Do you visit Waterloo often?"

"We were there about three weeks ago—Cedar Falls, actually, to take my mother-in-law to a concert at UNI," I answered. "The Winter Dance Party."

The tall and slender librarian's dark brown eyes lit up like a Christmas tree. "Oh, I love Buddy Holly!"

I tried to guess her age and of course didn't want to ask. I guessed she was about thirty-five at the very oldest. "Stacey, I'm working on a Buddy Holly project now. How is it that you're a fan at your young age?"

"How can you not be?" Stacey asked with more enthusiasm than I was expecting. "His influence on music is so extensive. I've read every book I can find on him and I've become a devoted fan of his music."

We both began talking enthusiastically about our mutual interest, stepping on each other's words as we did so. I found it so intriguing that she was so passionate about the same subject.

"My mother-in-law's husband said that he appeared at Electric Park in Waterloo and . . ." before I could finish Stacey interrupted me.

"Oh! There's a picture of him wearing sunglasses sitting on a freezer there. He is so handsome!"

Is? "He is so handsome." She had spoken in the present tense. To Stacey, Buddy still lives and is forever twenty-two.

"Yes. I know that picture," I responded. Stacey and I looked at each other. We had an instant connection. We were kindred spirits in our love of a man neither one of us have ever met and never will.

Stacey continued. "I remember seeing one of the first pictures of Buddy when I was young. I said, 'Dad, he looks like a nerd!' My dad shot back with great sincerity, 'Oh no, Stacey, he was cool.'" Stacey's love for Buddy Holly had been passed from father to daughter.

"'Peggy Sue' is my favorite song," Stacey continued. "It was originally named after the Crickets' drummer's girlfriend, but initially it was called 'Cindy Lou' after Buddy's niece and had a Caribbean sound. The drums were so loud in the recording studio that they put the drummer, Jerry Allison, out in the lobby. Jerry played paradiddles, and the sound of the drums is wavelike and undulating because they sent the sound into an echo chamber and turned the echo effect off and on."

The depth of her knowledge floored me. I'm a drummer and I was surprised Stacey knew what a paradiddle was and could identify it on an old Buddy Holly recording.

"Tell me more."

Stacey Cisneros, the Head of Adult Services at the Batavia (Illinois) Public Library, has been a Buddy Holly fan for most of her life. *Author*

Stacey's eyes positively glowed with excitement. "This is my favorite fact of all!" she exclaimed. "Buddy played both lead and rhythm guitar on the recording. The other guitarist in the Crickets at the time knelt next to Buddy in the studio to flip a switch on Buddy's guitar so he could make a smooth transition into the guitar solo!"

I was blown away. This attractive young librarian with the lovely ash-blonde hair was no casual fan. She knew her Buddy Holly history and she knew it in great detail. I didn't yet know any of these facts, but there wasn't much I knew at that point in my pursuit of Buddy Holly.

And then the mood changed. Her brown eyes saddened as the smile left her face. Her body language changed, too. She began fidgeting as if physically uncomfortable.

"What's wrong, Stacey?" I asked.

"I have always felt guilty," Stacey continued, sighing as she looked away from me. "It happened in my state. Not just in my state but close to home. My part of the state. My quadrant."

Stacey somehow felt responsible. It was interesting, even charming in a strange sort of way. She shouldered part of the responsibility in the same way a Texan might about the assassination of JFK. Iowans and Buddy Holly seem forever connected, not only by the tragedy but by the proximity of the loss. The music that Don McLean sang about dying died in their backyard. I remembered the thirty-something librarian in Independence, Iowa, who stopped me as I was leaving only to tell me that Buddy died there. Stacey was about the same age.

I know an Iowa girl when I see one. I'm married to one. Stacey is an Iowa girl from head to toe. She regrets that Buddy crashed and died in Iowa, leaving Mason City aboard an Iowa charter flight, flown by an Iowa pilot. She looks at the picture of Buddy taken in Iowa and feels terrible about the fact that he left this life in her state.

Stacey turned back to look at me. "When I was very young and a small plane would fly overhead, my dad would look up and say, 'Stacey, that plane is owned by Dwyer's Flying Service. That's the company who owned the plane Buddy Holly died in.' That's what he would tell me." This father's words profoundly impacted his daughter.

My mind wandered, as it is prone to do. I imagined a little blonde girl wearing a sundress standing in her Iowa backyard next to her father, a Barbie doll in one hand and the other shading her eyes from the sun. There is a light breeze. Father and daughter are both looking up to see the plane her dad is pointing out. How could her father have ever imagined that that moment with Stacey would affect his little girl into adulthood and probably for the rest of her life? Stacey is now forever gazing upward, remembering those words and the fateful event they represent.

The late great Buddy Holly sang his last song and strummed his guitar for the last time in Iowa. When he closed his guitar case that fateful night, no one could have imagined that it would be Buddy's good friend Waylon Jennings who would open the case with tears streaming down his cheeks. Buddy took his last breath and it was Iowa air that filled his lungs. His heart beat its last beat when his body slammed into the rich Iowa farm soil. People from all over the world travel to Iowa to pay homage to Buddy. They stand in a farm field near a stainless steel marker five miles north of Mason City and remember his music, last heard live on an Iowa stage.

Stacey is a very special person. She feels the weight of these facts every day.

I was blown away.

Chapter 11

But it starts raining in my heart

"Are you the guy trying to reach my husband?" demanded a female voice on the other end of the phone.

"I guess that depends," I laughed. The voice on the other end remained silent. "Who's your husband?"

"My name is Barb Dwyer. Jerry Dwyer is my husband."

The last name stunned me into silence. Everyone I knew living in and around Mason City and Clear Lake told me neither Dwyer would ever speak to me if the subject was related even remotely to Buddy Holly. Despite the friendly warnings I left a message on their answering machine. For me, "no" is simply the first step on the road to "yes." Then I called again. And again. As the days and then weeks slipped past I admit to losing hope that they would return my calls. And now, finally, Barb Dwyer was on the line.

"Yes, I have been trying to reach him," I answered when I pulled myself back to the present. "But I would like to talk to both of you, not just Jerry."

Jerry Dwyer and his wife Barb own and manage Dwyer Flying Services of Mason City, Iowa. On February 3, 1959, Jerry provided the chartered flight for Buddy, Ritchie, and the Big Bopper that was to fly the trio of musicians from Mason City to Fargo, North Dakota, for their scheduled performance in Moorhead, Minnesota. The flight was scheduled for late on the night of the 2nd or early on the morning of the 3rd. According to surviving records, the plane took off from the Mason City airport at 12:55 a.m. on February 3, 1959. Fewer than ten minutes later everyone on board was dead.

"I don't know that we want to talk to you," Barb replied. Her answer was curtly delivered.

"Well, you must want to talk because you called me back," I answered as gently as possible.

She paused for a few seconds as she mulled over my response. "If we did speak to you, what would we talk about?"

"I'm working on a Buddy Holly project. It's not a biography," I hastened to add. "I'm writing about how Buddy, his music, and his life have impacted, and continue to impact, the lives of others."

Several more seconds of silence passed. "Why do you want to talk to us?" she finally asked. "We have nothing to add."

I had been thinking for weeks about how to answer the obvious question I knew she would ask me. Would she hang up? Would she open up and talk with me? I decided to simply say it and let her decide. "Because I strongly suspect that the moment that plane went down, your lives were forever changed." An icy silence followed. When it became uncomfortably long, I added, "Am I wrong?"

Once again my words were followed by dead air. If I was a betting man, I would have wagered that the next sound I was going to hear was the "click" of her phone hanging up. Instead, I heard her clear her throat and continue. "We're very busy and may not be able to talk to you for months. Besides, Jerry is writing his own book."

"He is?" I replied. "That's great. I might be able to help you with it and I would even help you find a publisher, if you like . . ."

"You know," she interrupted, "the truth has never come out about that flight. Jerry will tell the truth because the truth has never been told." Her voice was cold and defiant.

The conversation had taken a sudden and unexpected turn. "The truth? What is the truth, Barb?" I asked. When she didn't answer I added,

"I would love to give you the conduit to deliver the truth, but honestly Barb, the focus of this book is more about how you were impacted by your brush with Buddy Holly than it is about the event itself."

What was the truth that has never been told?

I confess I was dying to hear the "truth" according to Barb and Jerry Dwyer, but I was worried that pushing the issue would risk losing the opportunity to speak with them about what I really wanted to know.

The last thing I wanted was for her to hang up, so I kept talking. I shared with Barb my experience as a pilot, and that for a few years I had operated the flight school and air charter service at the Kankakee Valley Airport (IKK). The common experience between us warmed the conversation, and I sensed Barb loosening up a bit.

"It's not an easy business," she said.

"It is a very difficult and stressful way to make a living," I admitted, breathing an inner sigh of relief. She was still talking. After discussing various aviation issues, I thought of something else that might help her feel comfortable about speaking with me.

"Did you know we have a mutual friend?"

"We do?" She sounded surprised. "Who's that?"

"John Skipper." John is a veteran newspaper man with the Mason City *Globe Gazette*. He read and helped edit the baseball portions of my first book.

"Oh, yes. We know John."

It was time to circle back around to the main issue. "Barb, I'm on a short deadline."

"How short?" she asked.

"Very short," I responded. "I'm really out of time, but I can get my publisher to hold the presses if you will talk with me."

"We maybe can talk in the Fall," she offered. "Maybe not." It was already late July.

"That won't work for us," I explained. "My deadline is the middle of August, and we really need to speak soon. Is Jerry available now?" I asked. Was I was pushing my luck?

"He's out of town," she replied. "We're selling off our aircraft and retiring. We have to have all the planes out of Mason City soon, so we are really busy." Her answer was once again clipped, curt.

"I can arrange a conference call and we can get him on wherever he is," I offered.

"No," Barb said firmly. "I'll get back to you in a couple of days." A second or two of silence followed before she added, "You want to know how Buddy Holly impacted our lives?"

"Yes," I replied.

"Buddy Holly ruined our lives." And without so much as a goodbye she hung up.

I pulled the phone from my ear and said aloud, "Wow. I could can understand that. And what truth about that night has never been told?"

Barb Dwyer was trying to tell me she and her husband know something about the flight and the accident that has never been disclosed.

Is that even possible?

Chapter 12

When I think of all you had

"For three days a year I am the most famous photographer in the world! That's how Buddy Holly has impacted my life," he responded over the phone without hesitation.

Dick Cole of Waterloo, Iowa, is forever a part of Buddy Holly's enduring legacy, and his brush with the legend changed his life forever. "That few moments in the kitchen in the ballroom at Electric Park in the summer of 1958," Dick reminisced, "set my life on a course I could never have anticipated or planned."

Arguably, Dick snapped the most famous Buddy Holly picture ever taken. At that time he was a seventeen-year-old photographer on staff at the Waterloo *Courier*. His employer didn't condone this new type of music that was sweeping the country and moving and shaking the young of America. As a result, that night Dick paid a visit to the Electric Park Ballroom on his own—as a fan. His expectations were modest. He wanted to take a few pictures for his private collection. But that night, Dick caught lightning in a bottle.

According to Buddy's widow, Maria Elena Holly, Dick's snapshot captures Buddy better than any other photo in existence. And because Buddy fans all over the world are familiar with the photograph, they know the name Dick Cole.

Dick Cole with his ubiquitous camera. For a few days each year he is arguably the most popular photographer in the world. *David Wieland*

"I was a big Buddy Holly fan and of Rock & Roll in general," Dick admitted. "I was young and completely taken by the whole musical movement. We were lucky in Waterloo to get the biggest acts in the business, but always on week nights. Waterloo is situated between larger venues and the big cities hosted Holly and others on weekends, so we caught them as they passed through. If you were in Minneapolis one weekend and Kansas City the next, for example, the acts could play Wednesday night in Waterloo and pick up an extra five hundred bucks during the week!"

Each year during the first three days of February, newspapers and magazines across the nation and around the globe publish Cole's picture and often call to interview him.

"Nearly every reporter asks me same question," he told me. "They want to know, 'What were you thinking the moment you snapped that famous photograph?'"

"What else do they ask you about?" I inquired.

"Everyone asks what we talked about and I really don't remember in any detail," Dick answered. He could have made something up, but that's just not Dick Cole. "He was so friendly and kind. We made small talk and I felt like I was talking to a friend," he continued. "In fact, Buddy did make friends in Waterloo and even went water skiing the next day with local fans. Buddy promised to come back the next summer for a few days to vacation but of course, he was not around to make his promised return."

"That one photo made you famous around the world," I continued.

"Yes, it did." Dick shared a story with me to confirm my observation. "I was at the Surf Ballroom for one of the anniversaries. I can't remember which. The forty-fifth maybe, I don't know," he said. "I got out of the car and was mobbed by a group of Japanese tourists yelling, 'Famous photographer Dick Cole!' I had to pose for pictures with each one of them. I'm more famous in Japan than my hometown. Can you believe it?" He paused for a moment.

"I was there for the fiftieth anniversary in 2009, but on February 2, 1959, I couldn't make the concert at the Surf. I was working at the newspaper and we were at the peak of the Iowa basketball season. I was on a basketball floor capturing the action that night, but my heart and mind were in Clear Lake. I was just sick over what I knew I was missing." Dick paused and thought for a moment. "There were so few pictures taken that last night. Had I been there, I would have captured it all on film." He laughed. "Maybe then I would have been famous for more than three days!"

One of the photos Dick Cole captured of Buddy Holly that night so long ago at Waterloo's Electric Park Ballroom. *Dick Cole*

Chapter 13

Hey, Buddy. I got those early in the morning blues

I had not worked on *Hey Buddy* for a few days. I needed a break from the emotional involvement in this project that was consuming me in a strange and complicated way. But tonight I decided to dig in and get back to work, so I spent my evening going back and forth between Dick Cole's photo of Buddy and YouTube.com, watching Buddy Holly and John Mueller. I was drawn to the videos people from all over the world posted to document their pilgrimages to the crash site. I needed to visit Clear Lake. A variety of musical artists on YouTube freely talk about how Buddy influenced their music and lives. I got it. He was certainly impacting mine.

I found a tape recording online of Buddy in a phone conversation with a recording executive who was holding some of Buddy's unreleased songs. Buddy wanted him to give up his rights to the songs so he could re-record them elsewhere. The executive refused without providing a good reason. He also refused to make any promises that they would ever be released, which must have frustrated and disheartened Buddy.

The more I listened to this record executive, the angrier I became. I think most people would feel the same way. I wanted to snap back at him, "How dare you!"

But not Buddy.

According to the people who knew Buddy the best, he never angered and he never used a harsh word. He was kind and patient even in the face of a man who stood between him and his music. This recording is a perfect example of the Buddy that Gary and Ramona spoke so lovingly about. I think again about Stacey the librarian and her conversations with her dad. I listened again to the beginning of "American Pie," over and over. Then John Mueller singing "Hey, Buddy." To my surprise, I began to cry.

I was so happy my mother-in-law and John Mueller introduced me to Buddy Holly, and yet at the same time I felt the deep sadness for the loss of a friend I never met. What was happening to me? This was so odd . . . so very strange. This wasn't like me.

I have found that as I get older I cry more easily, but how can I feel this loss for someone I never met who has been dead for more than five decades? I felt it, but I don't "get" it.

I conducted Twitter searches every hour or so today. Twitter is an Internet social networking tool that allows users to send out short messages ("tweets") to those who follow them. Today I was searching twitterers around the world for anyone using "Buddy Holly." To my surprise, roughly ten to twenty-five tweets per hour mentioned his name. Some mentioned a song they were listening to at that moment—"Listening to 'Everyday.' Oh boy, I miss Buddy Holly." Others asked rhetorical questions: "Was anyone ever better than Buddy?" Many tweets were from radio stations announcing what Buddy song they were playing at that moment. Someone posted on my Facebook page: "Listening to Buddy Holly on my way to work. Perfect way to start my day!" Another offered a more profound observation when he wrote, "Buddy Holly was 52 years ahead of his time and we are still left trying to catch up." I suspected there was a lot of truth in that last one.

"Buddy Holly died on my nineteenth birthday, February 3, 1959," Gene Onesto, a fellow alumnus of the Cavaliers Drum & Bugle Corps, posted on our alumni website. "It forever put a stamp on that day. Buddy Holly is a big part of the soundtrack of my life."

I spoke at Lincoln-Way High School today as part of National Library Week. Someone asked me if I was working on a new book. "I am," I replied. "A Buddy Holly project." Everyone in the room turned to look at a fifteen-year-old boy in glasses. My eyes followed their gaze. "Are you a Buddy Holly fan?" I asked.

"Yes," was his short and only response.

I finished my talk and signed a few books. I looked up to see the young Buddy fan waiting at the end of the line. We locked eyes and I smiled.

"My name is Mike W—. I love Buddy Holly," he blurted out. His expression conveyed that he was embarrassed by his outburst.

"Why?" I asked

"His music speaks to me in ways no other music does." Sincerity and innocence echoed in his young voice. "I like old Rock & Roll, but Buddy Holly is . . . different." He paused. "I don't know what else to say." I believed him. He seemed embarrassed that he could not explain why, but his attraction to Buddy and his music was apparent.

Everywhere I go I've discovered a devotion, dedication, and passion for Buddy and his music. Yet, no one has really been able to put into words why they feel so devoted to Holly. John Mueller certainly feels it. Don McLean obviously did. Paul McCartney talks about it. Stacey the librarian feels a deep attachment to Buddy, as does this high school student.

What is it about this man that has strangers talking about him, listening to his music, and sending his name into cyberspace more than 50 years after his death? Buddy touched something. No, that's not quite right. Buddy still touches something. Don McLean put it best: "Something touched me deep inside, the day the music died." I was beginning to understand because Buddy has reached out and touched me.

And then I began to wonder: did I live through something important and miss it entirely? How did I miss out on one of America's most musically significant periods? Buddy and his Rock & Roll pioneer colleagues were making history and I blinked and missed it! And all the music during the entire decade that followed his death? A real sense of anxiety coursed through me. I'm not the only person of my generation who is musically challenged when it comes to Rock & Roll—am I? How can I write about this if I cannot put it into words?

Why did I ignore or turn away from the music of my youth? I decided to keep searching, but what, exactly, was I searching for?

Chapter 14

I'm gonna set my foot right down

It was a hot day in Columbus, Ohio, and John Mueller's "Winter Dance Party" was on the grounds performing that evening with the Columbus Symphony at their "Picnic with the Pops" concert. I checked the Weather Channel app on my iPhone: 95 degrees, with a severe heat advisory all day. Great.

I flew into Columbus that morning with enough time to catch the last half of the rehearsal but the band cut it off early because of the intense heat. I hailed a cab and headed to the Chemical Abstract Services (CAS) facility at 2450 Olentangy River Road. The summer concert series was on the beautiful lawn of the CAS building. I didn't know who CAS was or what they did, but trying to get into the building to meet John was like trying to get into the Pentagon. (I say this as if I have ever tried to get into the Pentagon, which I have not.) Regardless, security was high. Eventually I produced enough ID and signed enough forms to give the reference from John himself sufficient credence to secure me an escort to the cafeteria to meet him and his band for the first time.

John Mueller had been living in my head next to Buddy for nearly six months. I'd seen his show, watched him on YouTube, and listened to his voice in my car each day singing "Hey, Buddy." We had exchanged

Ray Anthony (left), John Mueller (center), and T. J. Dawson (right, filling in for Jay Richardson during his recovery from heart surgery), getting ready to go on stage for another fabulous show. *Author*

countless emails and spoken on the phone. I felt as though I knew him fairly well. Still, seeing him in the flesh the first time felt a bit strange.

John was gracious with his time and introduced me to his band and to Ray Anthony, who portrays Ritchie Valens. Jay Richardson, Big Bopper's son, was home recovering from open heart surgery so T. J. Dawson was performing in his place. Everyone was friendly and relaxed. As we made small talk I realized that many of the questions I had prepared to ask were not really that useful, so I decided to just sit back and let the chatter sweep us along at its own pace.

The group told me of the immense heat on stage during their rehearsal, what traveling and life on the road was like, and a host of other things. I caught a ride with them back to their hotel and John and Ray set aside some time to talk with me. The hotel was across from the Ohio State University football stadium on the campus of OSU. I'm not an OSU fan but my friend Tim Duggan is a University of Michigan alumnus. The Ohio State Buckeyes and the University of Michigan Wolverines are bitter rivals, so I quickly snapped a picture of the OSU stadium and sent it to him as a text message under the title, "Where Wolverines Come to Die." I smiled and mumbled to the doorman, "That'll irritate him all day."

We walked into the plush Blackwell Hotel, found a secluded area of the lobby complete with overstuffed leather chairs and dark wood accents, and made ourselves comfortable. Suddenly I felt awkward, almost silly for wasting their time just because I had developed an interest—or an obsession—in Buddy Holly. "Thank you so much for your time," I began. "I don't want to be in the way today. If you don't mind, I'd like to just hang out and see what you do for show prep and maybe ask a few questions and talk about anything that comes to mind. Anything you think is helpful for me to know, you tell me. Is that okay?"

"Sure, no problem," John responded with a smile.

When I told Ray how much I enjoyed his performance in Cedar Falls, his eyes brightened. "I love what I do for a living, and portraying Ritchie is a privilege," he answered enthusiastically. I learned that he communicates often with Ritchie's family and finds it an honor to keep his music alive. There was real emotion in his eyes. He meant every word.

When I casually mentioned that he had performed Ritchie's music hundreds, maybe thousands of times more than Ritchie Valens, Ray's mouth fell open. He looked at me, then John, and then back at me, "Wow. That had never occurred to me. I guess I have."

John smiled knowingly. "Gary said that same thing to me several months ago and it really made me think," he said. "It certainly puts what we do in a different perspective."

John and Ray are a different kind of performer than Jay and his understudy for the night, T.J., and I think it is this longevity that sets them apart. Jay is the Big Bopper's son and he is carrying on a family tradition of sorts. I suspect Jay's motivation is different than the others. John and Ray hold onto the traditions of Buddy and Ritchie, but I think they interpret more than they imitate. I shared this idea with John and Ray and they agreed.

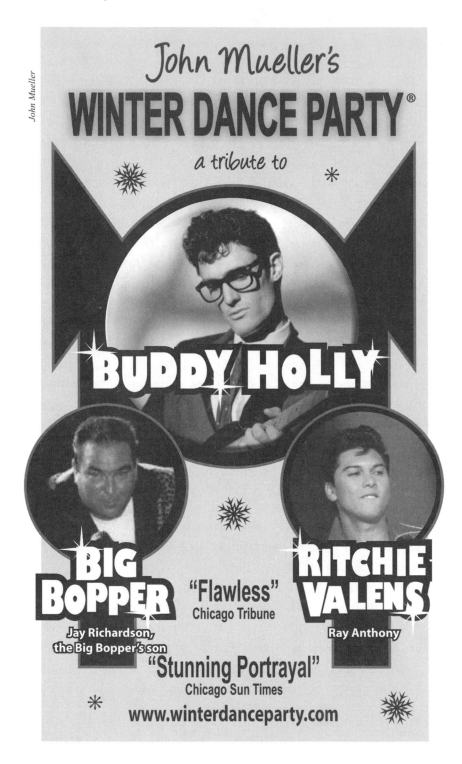

"I think we stopped trying to be carbon copy imitators years ago," replied John. "We work hard to keep the music alive and introduce it to a new audience, but with our own twists, with our own personalities." John paused before adding, "I think you're right, Gary. Tonight we are performing with the Columbus Symphony. When they are not playing old time Rock & Roll with us, they are playing Beethoven, Mozart, and Bach. Are they Beethoven imitators?"

"No," I responded. "They are performing and interpreting the works of a great composer who is no longer with us."

"Aren't we doing the same thing?" John asked.

"I never thought of it in that light," Ray chimed in. "I do my best to stay true to the music and keep it moving for generations to come but yes, I like that. We interpret. I think that's right."

Ray began interpreting Ritchie Valens as part of the Legends performance in Las Vegas. A friend told him about John Mueller and he called and asked John to be part of the show. John agreed and the two have been performing together since 2001.

"How long do you want to keep interpreting Ritchie?" I asked Ray.

John and Ray looked at each other and laughed. "Every year, we say it is almost over. We're getting older, but every year the demand grows," explained Ray.

"It does indeed," added John. "The phone keeps ringing. There seems to be an increasing demand for this show. We're not complaining. We love doing this, but we also know the day will come where we'll turn it over to some younger guys who can be as passionate as we are."

"But you are younger guys!" I responded.

"Well, Ritchie was only seventeen when he died and Buddy was just twenty-two," John replied. "We are well past those ages."

"So I guess part of your interpretation might be what Ritchie and Buddy would have been like had they lived a few years longer," I suggested. "But from the audience's perspective, you do twenty-two and seventeen perfectly. Trust me. I've seen it." We all laughed.

"Let me ask you a different question. Do you ever have identity confusion?" I wasn't sure if they would understand the point of my inquiry. They did.

"No, not really," John responded with a shake of the head. "Former Cricket Nikki Sullivan gave me some great advice when I was getting started. He said, 'Don't let the glasses consume you.' I understood what he was saying and took it to heart. Besides, I'm an actor and a musician. I play the music of others, as well as compose and perform my own music. I'm also an actor and do other roles and personalities."

The conversation continued and after a while I could see John's eyes beginning to narrow and his head nodding slightly. He and his band had traveled the night before and had just finished a shortened but intense rehearsal under a hot sun. "I'll let you guys get some rest and catch you tonight at the venue."

*   *   *

About 5:30 p.m. I decided to leave the hotel early and walk the mile or so to the concert site. I needed the exercise and it would be fun to watch the band and crew prepare for the show.

I wondered how many people would turn out for an outside concert in this heat. The concert was billed as a symphony event called "Picnic with the Pops." John and his entourage were performing with the Columbus Symphony Orchestra, so I expected an older crowd and, with this heat, a smaller one at that. I was still hundreds of yards away from the venue when I noticed cars backed up in every direction and people standing in line at every entrance.

And then it dawned on me. The security was tight and the good folks at the venue did not give me the promised ID before I left. Shoot! Would they let me in? I had been there this afternoon, so I could talk my way in, right?

There were several entrances and the line closest to the building stretched about as far as the eye could see. I moved to the front and found a young woman with short hair and "Carla" printed in big letters on her name tag.

"Hi Carla!" I began with my biggest smile. "I'm with the band." That was fun to say, but it sounded silly and we both knew it.

"I bet you are," Carla responded slowly. "But they'll just have to go on without you tonight unless you can produce the proper badge."

"Badges? We don't need no stinking badges!" I laughed.

She didn't. Instead, she crossed her arms and said, "Actually, a stinking badge is necessary if you think you're going in there." She unfolded her arms and lifted one hand with her thumb pointing over her left shoulder.

"Carla, do I look like I am up to no good?" I replied, my wide smile still in place. "I don't even know what they do in that building."

"Let me get Marsha," Carla said, "But don't make a move toward the building or I'll drop you like a sack of potatoes." I started to laugh but the look on her face told me she was deadly serious. She returned a minute later with another woman about the same age with blonde hair and deep brown eyes. "Marsha, this guy says he's with the band," Carla offered in a skeptical voice. Marsha didn't say a word. Instead, she just looked at me and smiled. And kept smiling.

I cleared my throat and began. "Hi Marsha. My name is Gary W. Moore. I'm an author and John Mueller invited me to hang out and view things from backstage tonight." I handed Marsha my business card, which prominently features the cover of my first book, *Playing with the Enemy*. "I'm writing about Buddy Holly's enduring impact and how John Mueller and his Winter Dance Party are keeping his music alive."

Marsha looked at the card and then back up at me. "You wrote this book?" she asked, pointing to the cover art on the back of my card. "I know who you are. My son slept with this book for a month."

I let out an audible sigh. "Yes, I'm the author of that book." I wanted to stick my tongue out at Carla but managed to resist the urge. "I'm delighted your son enjoyed it. Have you read it?" I asked.

"No, sorry. But I'll take you in the building if you'll sign this card for my son," Marsha offered as she took my arm and began escorting me toward the door.

"Deal!" I answered, unable to resist the urge to look back at Carla and smile. "Why is security so high here, Marsha?" I asked, turning back to look at my escort.

"Ah, this is the Chemical Abstract Services building," she responded with raised eyebrows.

"Yes, but what do they do here and what are they protecting?" I asked.

"This building houses more detailed information on chemicals than any other site in the world. If it's a chemical, they have detailed information and formulas here."

"Oh, so they're afraid someone's going to steal the recipe for making Lysol?" I laughed. Marsha did not. None of these people seemed to have a sense of humor.

"I think they are concerned that something more harmful could fall into the wrong hands," she replied with deadly earnest. "I'm sure you understand. The world is a dangerous place today and some of what they store here might be of interest to those who wish to do us harm."

"Yes, of course," I said. "That was my feeble attempt at humor."

"Mission accomplished," she answered—and then broke into laughter. "It was feeble." We both laughed at that.

We walked into the building and Marsha guided me to security, where they took down all my information before handing me a badge. "I'm official now?" I asked Marsha.

"You are as official as you are going to get." She changed gears and asked me about the new project. After I explained why I was researching and writing it, she responded with a shrug. "I really don't know much about Buddy Holly, but you really are with the band. Have fun!" Marsha walked a few steps and then turned back to face me. "If I can get my son down here with his book, would you sign it?"

"I would be delighted, Marsha. I'll be hanging around the stage tonight so just look me up."

No one was in the dressing area or green room yet, but I could see a crowd gathering outside. I estimated the number at 3,000 and it was still quite early. As much as I hated to leave the air conditioning, it made sense to walk outside and talk to some folks to see why they were there.

The first person to cross my path was a woman with two teenagers carrying a picnic basket and lawn chairs. "Excuse me," I said. "What brings you out to the concert tonight?"

The crowd begins to gather for the Columbus show. *Author*

"What do you mean?" asked the mother.

"My name is Gary and I'm working on a Buddy Holly book. I'm curious as to why you took your time to come out tonight?"

According to the thirty-something mom, her son was a big fan of Buddy Holly's music. "In the process of playing it all night, every night in his room, we've all become fans," she explained.

Her son stood beside her in a Led Zeppelin T-shirt. "How old are you?"

"Sixteen," he replied, shaking the dark hair out of his eyes. "I play the guitar and like to play Buddy's songs." His smile revealed a set of blue braces.

I pointed to his T-shirt. "They're a long way from Buddy."

"Not really," he responded. "You find a little Buddy in most Rock & Roll and these guys loved Buddy."

"I'm sure you're right," I replied as I jotted down his words. "What's your favorite Buddy song?"

"'Not Fade Away,'" he answered without a moment's hesitation.

"'Peggy Sue,'" said his younger teenaged sister.

I looked at Mom and raised my eyebrows. "'That'll Be the Day!' Is my song," she said as she laughed and put her arm around her son's shoulders. "He's got us all hooked."

"You know what I think? Anything a parent and her children can enjoy and discuss together is a very healthy thing to be hooked on." I paused, again taking notes. "Have you seen this show before?"

"No," the young man answered. "But I've seen John Mueller on YouTube and he's the best."

That really got my attention. "Have you heard his song or seen his tribute video entitled 'Hey, Buddy?'" I asked.

"Oh yeah, that's my favorite. I cried the first time I listened to the words," admitted Mom.

"Me, too," I mumbled.

Mom and I exchanged knowing glances as I thanked them for their time and input and headed back inside to see if I could find John, Ray, T.J. and some air conditioning.

John is a very generous man and allowed me complete access backstage. As I knew it would be, the concert was outstanding. The crowd loved the music and showmanship. The evening could not have been more perfect. Just as he had in Cedar Falls, Iowa, near the end of the show John announced that he would conclude the evening with a song he had written as a tribute to Buddy. As much as I wanted to watch John perform his tribute song, I was there to watch the audience and register their reaction to the song. Was I the only one struck by the lyrics and music of this special tune?

"Hey, Buddy . . . Look at me . . . I'm just sitting here reminiscing . . . "

There is still something hypnotic about that song no matter how many times (or where) I hear it. I forced myself to turn away from the stage and focus on the faces in the crowd.

The audience had been dialed in all evening, and nothing changed when John started playing his own original music. I did see something very interesting, however. A group of about thirty audience members off on the side of the stage had been dancing non-stop for the entire show. A few measures into "Hey, Buddy" they stopped—almost as one—and

John Mueller performing in Columbus. *Author*

began swaying back and forth, their eyes riveted on John as they listened to the song. In an odd sort of way I was looking backward in time. Something about it had captured me, and now it was capturing them. In a way I felt like a voyeur, watching and listening to John sing not to us, but to Buddy. Wait. That's not really right. John did speak to us: "Listen to me . . ." "Look at me . . ." I found it struck a perfect chord with my emotions and those of the audience.

"Hey Buddy . . . I'll see you . . . on down the line."

The haunting words faded away, the melody came to an end, and the audience fell silent—and for a brief moment my heart skipped a beat: Was something wrong?—before erupting into enthusiastic applause.

The audience cheered as John, Ray, T. J., the Winter Dance Party Band, and the Columbus Symphony Orchestra took the stage to bow together to a rousing standing ovation. The evening was an unqualified success. John and entourage made for the souvenir-autograph table, where hundreds of people poured themselves into a chattering line to acquire a CD, a signed photo—anything to help keep alive this thoroughly memorable evening. I assumed a position a few feet off to the side of the table area in hopes of catching a few conversations.

"I've been coming to these summer events since they began," said Bill, a tall 65-year-old recent retiree with the thickest head of white hair I had ever seen. "Your performance tonight was incredible!" he told John as he leaned over and shook his hand. "I never miss one of these picnic concerts and tonight's was the best of all."

I corralled Bill for a few moments, explained my presence and purpose, and asked him to describe his musical tastes for me. He thought for a moment and then replied, "Let's put it this way. I was not a Buddy fan, but I am now!"

A middle-aged woman named Candy, who purchased a CD of John's music, attended that night with her 20-year-old son and his friend. The excitement written across their faces was obvious. When they began moving away from the table I walked up with my notepad and pen in hand and said, "Excuse me. May I have a moment of your time?"

"Sure," smiled Candy. "Are you with the newspaper?"

"No. Actually, I'm writing a book on the impact of Buddy's life. Are you a fan?" I asked.

She looked at me as if to say, "Are you crazy?" and then started bobbing her head up and down. "I am! Isn't everyone?"

"How about you?" I asked, looking at her son.

"Yeah. I listen to his music all the time," he replied.

"How did you become a fan?" I asked. This subject really interests me. The young man looked at his mom and smiled. "My mom listens to him and as I listened, I became hooked. Really hooked."

Mom shot a proud look at her boy, slipped her arm around his shoulder and pulled him close. This was the second time tonight I had seen a mom and son embrace because of Buddy Holly. She was proud they shared a similar love for the same musician. This music brings families together. And yet, the music that followed Buddy in the 1960s pulled families apart. What was the difference?

Listening to John was wonderful, and talking to fans was insightful and encouraging, but what was it like to have seen Buddy in person? I really needed to find someone who was there and heard Buddy Holly live. Even better than that would be finding someone who was at The Surf for the last show on the last night.

I determined to begin that journey soon. Tonight I was in Columbus, Ohio, with 6,000 other people enjoying Buddy, Ritchie and the Big Bopper live on through John, Ray and T. J. As I witnessed firsthand on this very hot and muggy summer evening, even though the physical bodies are gone, the music raves on. Just as impressively, it is enjoyed and appreciated across generations. The energy that exists for Buddy and his music more than five decades after his physical life was extinguished leaves me in awe.

Chapter 15

On my valley of tears

"I arrived at the radio station early," Bob remembered as we spoke by phone. "I was the morning Rock & Roll disc jockey on KRIB AM in Mason City, Iowa. The night before was a late one. I had the honor, pleasure, and privilege of being the host and MC at The Winter Dance Party at the Surf Ballroom in neighboring Clear Lake. What a night!" he added before pausing as if in deep thought.

On the other end of the phone I did my best to try and imagine what Bob was feeling at that moment.

He cleared his throat and continued. "I went on the air at 10:00 a.m. the next morning, but arrived early to prepare for the show. The music was still swirling in my head. I pulled a report off of the wire service about a small plane crash north of Mason City but really never gave it a second thought. I just didn't put two and two together. Ten o'clock came and I was on the air, spinning records and reminiscing about how just the night before, the greatest assembly of contemporary musical talent in the world had been under one roof and here in our community. I met them, I talked to them, I interviewed them, and I hosted the show. Wow. It was an amazing night . . ."

Bob Hale is a broadcast legend, not only in Chicago where he spent the majority of his career, but nationwide. Buddy Holly and a few other musical pioneers transformed contemporary music while Bob Hale and

Broadcast legend Bob Hale, the morning Rock & Roll disc jockey on KRIB radio in Mason City, Iowa. *Bob Hale*

his visionary colleagues at WLS AM radio in Chicago—the 50,000 watt Clear Channel behemoth of broadcasting—transformed Rock & Roll radio.

As I noted earlier, I grew up in Kankakee, Illinois. I was 25 miles as the crow flies from the WLS tower in Tinley Park. All my friends listened to WLS, which owned Rock & Roll in the Midwest. Bob Hale, Dick Biondi, and a few others were the voices of the era and for thousands of listeners, the voices of their radio generation.

Bob continued his story for me. "About 10:10, Carroll Anderson called me at the station. Carroll ran the Surf Ballroom in Clear Lake, the venue that hosted The Winter Dance Party the night before," he explained. "I took the call. I don't remember what record was spinning, but I'm sure it was one of the performers from the night before. It was probably Buddy."

Here is how the conversation between Bob and Carroll unfolded:

"Bob, they're dead," Carroll said.

"What?" Bob asked. He didn't understand who Carroll was talking about. "Who's dead?"

"Their plane went down just north of town," Carroll continued with deep emotion in his voice. "They're all lying out in that corn field now. They're all dead, Bob."

Bob thought for a moment about who exactly was on the plane and then he understood. My God! Carroll was talking about Buddy Holly, Ritchie Valens, and the Big Bopper! "Are you sure it's their plane? Are you sure they're all dead?" asked Bob, hoping for a different answer.

Carroll confirmed the worst. "Yes. They're all dead. All of them."

"That must have been so horrible to hear," I replied after hearing the conversation that Bob had just described to me.

"I made the sorrowful announcement on the air," continued Bob. "I don't remember the exact words but I do remember the feeling of disbelief and loss. People immediately began arriving at the station. Kids left school and came directly to the studio. Some came alone. Some with friends. Others accompanied by their parents. There were so many tears. The sadness was overwhelming. That entire day turned into an on-air wake. I'll never forget February 3, 1959."

"Bob, can you share with me some of your memories and impressions of Buddy from the evening before?" I asked.

Bob was happy to do so. "The bus arrived late in the afternoon. It was a typical February day in Clear Lake. Very cold," he said. "They had continual mechanical problems with their chartered bus from the very beginning of the tour. They arrived without their drummer, Carl Bunch, who was left in Green Bay Wisconsin, hospitalized with frost bitten toes. The heater on the bus didn't work.

"From the moment the bus arrived, Buddy took charge. He directed the equipment set-up, discussed the upcoming evening event, discussed and decided performance order and did so while sitting at the piano, playing as he spoke. He was only twenty-two years old but possessed the leadership skills of a modern-day CEO. Buddy was clearly in charge of everything and everyone. It was equally apparent that those he led respected and liked him, while looking to him for direction.

"They didn't have a drummer so Buddy said he would play drums for the other acts that night if Ritchie would play for him. Buddy and Ritchie were the only two who could play the drums, so it was agreed. Can you imagine that happening today?" Bob asked. "Buddy was one of the biggest acts in Rock & Roll, but agreed to back up the others on drums. I think that speaks of his lack of ego and of his exceptional character. Buddy was all about getting the job done and doing whatever it took to do so.

"The tour director, Sam Gellar of General Artists Corporation, walked over to me and said, 'That guy,' pointing to Holly at the piano, 'is going to be the biggest influence in the history of the entertainment industry. He's not just a performer. He writes his own stuff and writes music for others. He produces his own records and runs the tour. Someday soon he will have his own recording studio, record label, and television show. We'll be working for him! He will be starring on the big screen, while writing and producing his own motion pictures. He can and will do it all. There is no one else like him that I've seen and I've been at this a long, long time.'"

"Do you think he was right?" I interjected.

"I do think Sam was right," replied Bob. "Buddy seemed to enjoy producing and writing for others as much as he did for himself. I think for Buddy, it was never about himself, but about the music and the creative process."

"And you witnessed all this firsthand . . ."

"In the short time he was in Clear Lake, Buddy directed set-up and preparation, played the piano, arranged for food to be brought for everyone, played the drums as part of the band for others, played and performed as the evening headliner and chartered a plane for later that night. He was destined to be 'Buddy, Inc,'" Bob continued, his voice suddenly filled with a lively energy as if he was anticipating the future rather than reliving one of the saddest memories of his life.

I remember thinking during this part of the conversation that Bob could be describing an early version of Oprah. I also thought about how the public persona of a very talented singer-songwriter in black glasses was only the tip of the iceberg. Buddy was so much more. He had the ability and drive to create an entertainment dynasty.

"The night began and there was a packed crowd at the Surf," Bob continued. "And not just teens but their parents, too. Carroll Anderson ran a good operation. He invited the parents to come to all the Rock & Roll shows, sometimes at a discount and sometimes for free. He supported this new music and wanted the parents there to see it was a good and wholesome event. The performers that night were Dion and the Belmonts, Ritchie Valens, J. P. 'Big Bopper' Richardson, Frankie Sardo, and of course, Buddy Holly. It was electrifying and the crowd at the Surf, parents and kids, loved every moment."

"Where were you during the show?" I asked.

"After Dion and the Belmonts performed, I sat on the front of the stage with Dion and asked him to introduce the band. One by one he called out their names and a little information about each of them. When it came to the drummer, Dion said, 'And here is our drummer . . . what's his name? His name . . . let's see. Well, his name is . . . Buddy Holly!' And with that, Buddy leaped out from behind the drums, where he had previously gone unnoticed, grabbed his guitar, and began playing 'Gotta Travel On,' a hit in 1958 by Billy Grammer, and the night roared to a climactic end with Holly as headliner."

Bob fell silent for a few moments. I so wished at that moment I could have shared his memories because he was vividly envisioning that night as he spoke. Bob didn't just witness history; he was a part of it.

"I'm often asked what was the last song Buddy performed that night. 'Brown Eyed Handsome Man' is the answer. The crowd begged for more. They yelled and screamed for an encore, but Buddy told them . . . he was running to catch a plane."

The phone was silent again for several seconds as Bob let the words sink in.

"How would you ever think that this would be his last performance, or that 'Brown Eyed Handsome Man' would be the last song he would ever sing? But as he walked off the stage that night, the unimaginable was about to happen, and the history of Rock & Roll was forever changed."

For a moment I felt like asking Bob why he didn't stop them from leaving for that plane. He was there! He could have changed everything! But of course, there was no way to know what was about to happen.

I changed the conversation to John Mueller and his impression of the legend.

"John Mueller is the closest thing to Buddy Holly that there can be," Bob confirmed. "He has him down pat and like Holly, John is a true gentleman. For me, John brings back all the memories of that night and the era. I've worked with John a few times and boy, does that bring back the emotions."

"Is there anything else you think I should know?"

"Buddy was clearly the star," Bob answered without hesitation. "He gets all the attention and he was the most popular of this tour, but don't cut Ritchie or the Big Bopper short. They were all talented and unique in their own special ways. Losing any one of them would have been a real tragedy and a loss for Rock & Roll, but to lose all of them in one night?

"Buddy Holly was so far ahead of us, not only in entertainment but in human relations. He traveled in a bus with African-Americans, something that in 1959 caused gasps from the masses. Buddy, a Baptist Texan, married a Puerto Rican Catholic. Maria Elena is a beautiful and wonderful woman, but in 1958 it was a bold step and an unlikely pairing. Buddy was way out in front of all of us in every part of his life."

The words conjured up the message someone had sent out via Twitter: "Buddy Holly was 52 years ahead of his time and we are still left trying to catch up." The tweet was perhaps more profound and accurate than its author realized.

"Buddy continued to be influential after his death. The Beatles say Buddy was their inspiration and that they modeled their early sound after him," explained Bob. "Now look at The Beatles' influence, not just musical influence but on modern culture! As good as The Beatles were, they stood on the shoulders of Buddy Holly. And you know, most people have no idea. Most people do not know. John Mueller and his Winter

Dance Party is introducing Buddy to a new generation and keeping the flame burning."

"How did Buddy Holly impact your life?" I asked.

"The fact I was the MC that last night in Clear Lake gave me instantaneous and national exposure. I moved quickly from Mason City to Chicago, with short stops in Springfield and Peoria," he explained. "I believe I would have made it to Chicago anyway, but I moved quickly because of my association with that last night at The Surf." Bob paused. "He was an amazing talent and a nice young man. I only met him once for a short but meaningful evening, but I will never forget him. Buddy was the real deal. It is impossible to fathom how far Buddy might have gone."

And where Buddy might have taken the rest of us, I wondered.

Chapter 16

I got nothing to lose

After speaking at length with Bob Hale about Buddy, I decided it would be a good idea to speak with a friend of mine who has been in the broadcasting business for many years.

I was late for our meeting when I walked into the French Toast Café a little after noon. As soon as I stepped inside I heard my name. "Gary! Over here," Tim Milner yelled from a table by the counter. I waved in acknowledgment and headed in his direction. "What do you think of this place?" he asked as we shook hands.

"Very cute," I replied. "Arlene would love this."

"They're an advertiser on our station," Tim explained. "I think they're doing well. Great food and atmosphere."

A charming thirty-something woman walked over and stood next to Tim. "Gary, this is Heather Lavine. She's the owner of French Toast Café," Tim said as he introduced me to the proprietor of the new establishment with the attractive French décor. "This restaurant is her dream." Heather walked us outside to show us the available seating she was preparing for later in the summer. When she left, Tim and I sat down to enjoy lunch.

Speaking with Bob Hale about radio in 1959 made me think about Buddy and radio today. Tim Milner is a radio man. He was born into the business and has never left it. His dad, Gene Milner, was legendary in

Philadelphia radio during the big band years. Being on the air wasn't enough for Gene, so he started buying radio stations. He ended up in Kankakee, Illinois, where he purchased a signal formerly known as WKAK FM and began broadcasting WBUS "The Bus" 99.9 FM. Gene and his family built "The Bus" from a start-up into one of Chicago's top stations. WBUS was 50,000 watts of top forty Rock & Roll and the only station my kids listened to when they were growing up. I was not a fan of the station's music, but I used to love their promos. On weekends they would play back-to-back hits without commercial interruption. Their deep-throated announcer, Ken Zyer, would come on and boom, "It's a double-decker weekend on the Buuuuusssssssss!" I listened on weekends just to hear that announcement. I don't know why, but it always made me laugh.

Tim's family sold WBUS years later and now owns WVLI "The Valley," WIVR "River Country," and WFAV, which simulcasts WVLI farther downstate Illinois. Tim also does radio consulting all over the country. Tim Milner knows radio. I asked him out to lunch to pick his brain about Buddy Holly and his impact, if any, on Tim's radio station—but did not tell him that in advance.

After talking for a few minutes about our families and work I moved on to the business at hand. "OK, Tim. What do you know about Buddy Holly?" I asked.

"An amazing artist and an amazing young man," Tim responded without a hint of hesitation. "He changed music." His eyes narrowed. "Why do you ask?"

"I'm working on a book about how Buddy's life has impacted, and continues to influence, others," I responded.

"A biography? I didn't know you were a fan!" Tim said.

"No. Not a biography," I quickly interjected. "It's more about his enduring legacy and its impact on other people and music. And no, I wasn't a fan . . . until recently."

"Okay," Tim shrugged. "What do you want to know?"

"Just start talking and use that as a general framework." I pulled out my pad and began taking notes.

Radio station owner Tim Milner. "People love Buddy Holly," he explained to me. "His music is almost ageless." *Author*

"Well, he was an incredible talent with a public career that lasted less than two years, but his impact has continued over the last . . . what . . . fifty years." Tim paused before asking, "What exactly are you looking for? I'm sure you already know that."

"I do. From the vantage point of a radio station owner, how do you look at Buddy Holly? Does he still influence your station in any way?"

"OK, I'm with you, Gary. Two things immediately come to mind," Tim answered as he turned his head and stared across the room. I had seen that look before. Tim chooses his words carefully. "We play a lot of Buddy on WVLI and we get a lot of calls from people under forty who ask who the artist is that we just played—or they'll ask if that was Buddy Holly. It never fails. People loved him in the late fifties, but an entirely new generation is discovering and learning to love him today. Let me put it this way," Tim continued. "It's good business to play Buddy."

"Does it surprise you to get calls from people who were not yet born when Buddy died?"

"No, not really," he answered with a determined shake of the head. "The music is good enough. It's almost ageless. People love Buddy Holly. And I love that song you casually suggested I listen to a few days ago . . . 'Hey, Buddy,' by John Mueller. Now I get why you wanted me to give it a listen." He smiled.

"I knew you'd like it," I grinned back. "Everyone who hears it, especially more than once, loves it."

"Then you'll like this," Tim continued. "We're going to use it to open or close our Buddy Holly set on the air. We'll use it opposite 'American Pie.' Open with one and close with the other, with Buddy sandwiched in the middle."

I nodded in agreement. "I do like it. You mentioned earlier that Buddy Holly is good for business. Why?" I asked. I knew the answer, of course, but wanted to hear Tim explain it.

"What comes out of that speaker in our listener's car, home, or business determines whether they stay tuned or tune us out. It can't just be good music. The quality of the recording has to be good, too. When we play older music, we have to be careful what we choose. It may be a great song and a former hit, but if it was poorly recorded or produced, I can't put it on the air regardless of what the song is or who the artists are."

"I had never really thought about that," I answered. "How does that relate to Buddy?"

"Digitally remastered is a term you often hear regarding older recordings," Tim explained. "Most Rock & Roll recordings from the fifties and into the early sixties were poorly produced. They sounded like they were recorded in a phone booth and the truth is, they almost were. But Buddy's stuff is perfect."

"What do you mean, perfect? How so?"

"That young man knew how to put it together with the skill of a master," answered Tim. "There's no need to digitally remaster or enhance a Buddy Holly-produced recording. They are technical works of art. You can't make them better. I think Buddy was a genius as a producer. He had the ear, imagination, and technical know-how to make it all fit in a unique and incredible way. No one else I know of from his era had that ability." Tim took a sip of iced tea before continuing. "At his age, limited experience, and lack of technical training and education . . ." Tim paused. "Somehow, someway, Buddy was able to produce recordings five decades ago that with today's technology cannot be improved upon."

Honestly, at that point I wasn't sure I believed him. Not that Tim would lie to me—he never would. But I had never heard what he just shared with me. Buddy was that far ahead of everyone else? Really? Surely Tim was exaggerating the quality of Buddy's recordings. With all the technology at hand today, we cannot take recordings more than five decades old, made by a twenty-something kid from Lubbock, Texas, and improve them?

"Hold up a second," I said. "Is that really true, or is it just Buddy legend or lore?" I asked. "You can't re-master or enhance it and make it better? With all of today's technical know-how . . . you cannot improve it?"

"Gary," Tim laughed, "It's that good. I don't know how, but it just is. With all our technology, can we improve upon the Mona Lisa?"

Was he saying that, like the paintings and sculptures that originated in the head of Michelangelo and then through his hands became the treasured works of art we enjoy today, Buddy Holly did much the same with his music? "No," I answered slowly. "You really can't improve on the Mona Lisa. And why would you when the original is perfect."

Buddy could hear the music in his head and recreate it on vinyl in a way that makes any attempt to tamper with it detract from the value of the original.

For Tim and his radio station, Buddy Holly is still good business.

Chapter 17

I start rocking around with Ollie Vee

February 3, 1959, is forever remembered as the day the music died. Don McLean memorialized the day as a riddle in a song for all the ages to hear, ponder, and sing along with. But if the music died, why is it so alive and vibrant today?

According to John Mueller, the demand for The Winter Dance Party is growing. Tim Milner says that in 2010, Buddy Holly's music is good business. In 2006, forty-seven years after Holly's death, "Not Fade Away" was performed by contestant Taylor Hicks on American Idol, one of the most popular television shows in history. Buddy is everywhere. Nothing about this seems dead to me. Buddy and his music seem very vibrant and alive.

I'm lying in bed. The clock says 3:16 AM. I can't sleep. I have Buddy and the day the music died on my mind. A strange thing begins rattling around in my head. According to the Bible, you must die and be reborn again to achieve eternal life. If the music died on that frozen Iowa field, it has certainly risen from the grave to enjoy life after death. Buddy seems to be as popular today, at least in some circles, as he was on February 2, 1959.

But what if he had lived? Would he still be as popular today? Would he be more popular?

Buddy died at the pinnacle of his young career, but he was still on his way up when he left us. Would his star have continued to rise, or would he have been inundated by the British wave spearheaded by The Beatles and the Rolling Stones and shoved off to one side to wither away?

It's warm in here. I pull my left leg outside of the covers in an effort to cool down. I think about my discussions with people who knew Buddy. Bob Hale certainly believes Buddy would have continued to soar and says so with conviction. He believes Buddy would have dominated every level of the entertainment business. I throw my covers off completely.

According to an author in a London newspaper article published on the 50th anniversary of the crash, Buddy would have veered toward Country and Western and transformed that genre the same way he transformed Rock & Roll. A few critics argue that Buddy's last few records were an indication that he was becoming more mainstream and less creative. I don't believe there is enough evidence to substantiate either claim. It's fun to speculate, but Buddy's career was so short and so intense that we are all left dreaming and guessing what might have been. It's not warm. It's hot in here. I can make out the blades of the ceiling fan in the dark. Why aren't they moving?

This is nuts. I can't sleep. I get out of bed and go into the family room and turn on the television, but I'm still thinking about Buddy. He was different from the other rockers. He was committed to his faith and did not believe in drugs. Buddy smoked cigarettes, but nearly everyone did back then. According to John Wayne and other celebrities, seven out of ten doctors smoked their brand. Who can argue with the Duke? Oh, and Buddy didn't drink alcohol, either.

The women who knew him all say the same things. "He was so kind," or "He was so humble," or "He was such a gentleman." Is there no one out there with a cross word to say about Buddy?

I turn on my TV to the History Channel just as the program cuts to a commercial. Buddy's "Everyday" is the background song. I laugh and shake my head. A few months ago I would not have been able to recognize the artist or the song. Now it seems as if I can't escape Buddy—even in the middle of the night in my family room. He is woven into the fabric of our nation and much of the world, and now, finally, into my life. How many people truly realize that?

Maybe a glass of milk will help me sleep. I head into the kitchen and open the refrigerator door. Buddy was so far ahead of the rest of us in every way. Musically, of course, but what about socially? There's only enough milk for Arlene's coffee in the morning. I'll try the lemonade. I'm reminded again of my interview with Bob Hale. According to the legendary DJ, Buddy rode on a bus with black Americans in the 1950s—a bold and unusual move for anyone back then, and especially a Texan. As a Baptist he married a Catholic Puerto Rican. Today these things are so inconsequential they don't even merit a comment. But for a 1950s white Baptist Texan, these facts are most extraordinary. Buddy was indeed so far ahead of the rest of us that we are still trying to catch up. I head back to the couch with my lemonade, wishing it was milk.

The more I learn about the history and progression of Rock & Roll, the more I understand the significance of February 3, 1959. The sudden and unexpected loss of Buddy, Ritchie, and the Big Bopper dramatically and significantly changed the course of contemporary music and American culture. The crash knocked America out of the oncoming rush of Rock music and left the doors wide open for the British to conquer. The crash left a void in the progression of the art of American music. How different would it all have been if Buddy had lived?

I hear the pitter-patter of paws and look up to see our golden retriever Noah. "Can't sleep either, huh boy?" Noah pushes his nose under my hand, begging to be stroked. How can I resist?

I remember Jim Riordan told me once that writing *Break on Through*, his book on Jim Morrison, nearly killed him. Thinking and writing about Buddy isn't killing me in any sense of the word, but it has consumed all of the gray matter between my ears and left little room there for anything else.

I look up at the ceiling and say aloud, "Buddy, can you give me a pass tonight? Please? I really need to sleep. I promise I'll pick up where we left off tonight in the morning!"

My pleadings with a ghost are interrupted by the bedroom door opening. I look over and see Arlene standing there, leaning against the door frame with her arms crossed.

"Buddy?" she asks.

"Yes," I answer, feeling embarrassed.

She smiles and extends her hand. "It's Arlene's turn. Buddy will have to wait."

Good night.

Chapter 18

Everyday

He was fifteen way back then, and Robert Thomas Velline was looking forward to February 3, 1959, with youthful enthusiasm. The Music was coming to Moorhead, Minnesota, just across the river from his hometown of Fargo, North Dakota. He and his friends had tickets to see Buddy Holly's "Winter Dance Party" at the National Guard Armory. For Robert, waiting was simply painful. Days passed like weeks and minutes like hours as he and his friends anticipated the arrival of their teen idols.

The Vellines were a musical family. Robert's father Sidney played the piano and violin, and Robert's two brothers, Bill and Sidney Jr., played the guitar. Robert played in the high school band, but he found the formality of the band inhibiting.

"I played saxophone in the high school band," remembers Robert, "But I wanted to rock out. We were playing all the standard band pieces and I wanted to do 'Yakety Yak.' My brother Bill went out and bought a guitar and I saved up enough money from my paper route to eventually buy a new (but sun faded) thirty dollar Harmony guitar for myself. We took advantage of each and every opportunity to see any musical act we could. Fargo hosted a lot of Country and Western acts," he continued. "We would attend, listen, and then come home afterward and do our own version of the show in the living room of our home."

But that was Country and Western. On February 3, 1959, Rock & Roll was coming to Moorhead and Robert, along with his brothers, friends, and every other teenager in the area, was looking forward to the arrival of The Winter Dance Party, featuring their favorite musical sensation, Buddy Holly!

Robert remembers the day. In fact, he will never forget it:

"It was February 3, 1959. I was a sophomore in high school and only lived a few blocks from school. The talk that day was all about Buddy Holly and the Crickets, Ritchie Valens, the Big Bopper, and Dion and the Belmonts. We could not believe they were coming to town. Our town!

"I ran home to have lunch and my mom was standing in the living room listening to the radio. Charlie Boone was on the air and I heard him mention The Winter Dance Party. My ears perked up, but I was not prepared for what I heard. How could it be? My heart had trouble accepting what my mind was processing.

"I was such a fan. Buddy Holly was in his very own zone, doing what he wanted to do and Buddy could do it all. He could write, perform, produce . . . we'll never really know the full extent of his talent and abilities.

"Rock & Roll was new and it was bonkers," Robert continued. "I was wild about it. We had a little garage band, one of only two in town. When I got back to school, Jim Stillman, our bass player, told me they were looking for bands to fill the void at the armory left by the death of the three artists. I still cannot believe they were going to put that show on, but they did. Jim called Charlie Boone at the radio station and said we would like to perform. To our surprise, Charlie said to show up, but to look good.

"We headed to JC Penney and bought matching shirts and ties and then headed straight for the armory. We were waiting in the wings backstage. I recognized Dion and the Belmonts and was looking for the Crickets when Charlie came up and asked for the name of our band. We'd never given it a thought! We looked at each other and it just popped out of my mouth: The Shadows!

"It happened quickly. We took our place on the stage and it was a surreal experience. There was the excitement we felt for getting this opportunity, along with the terrible realization that the slot to perform was only opened by the death of my hero, Buddy Holly."

"What was it like when you were about to play?" I asked.

"The curtains of the old armory stage opened, the spot light blinded me, and the show was on!" he explained. "I was so nervous, I really don't know how I made it to the microphone, but I did.

"We must have done well. A local agent and promoter gave us his card and said if we wanted some work, he could give it to us. We called him three days later and within three months we had twenty songs and were recording and selling records."

Robert was impacted by the life of Buddy through his musical influence. But he was also deeply impacted by Buddy's death, perhaps more so than the musician's short life. The downing of that charter plan left an opportunity for his band to perform, and on that night in Moorhead, Minnesota, 15-year-old Robert Velline and his garage band became Bobby Vee and the Shadows, known today for such hits as "Suzy Baby" and "Take Good Care of My Baby."

When speaking with Bobby on the phone, I kept thinking about how kind and humble he is. Now in the sixties, Bobby Vee is about as big as you can get yet it felt like I was talking to an old friend. It occurred to me that this is much the same way people described Buddy. Maybe Buddy's influence for Bobby is more than the music, and included an attitude and way of life.

"I still perform," Bobby continued. "We did a two and a half year run in Branson, Missouri, and had a ball. I keep going and keep reinventing myself. To stay alive in this business, it's what you have to do."

More than five decades later Bobby Vee still graces the airwaves of radio stations all over the world and is often heard back-to-back with his hero, Buddy Holly. Opportunity often rises from the ashes of tragedy, although there is little doubt in my mind that Bobby Vee would change the past if he had the chance to do so.

Buddy's impact on others is everywhere. Just ask Bobby.

Chapter 19

A rock-a-bye rock

"I love Buddy," intones a young female voice from Lincoln, Nebraska though my iPhone. "His voice is pure, sincere, and original. He never fails to make me happy. No matter what I'm doing or what is wrong in my life, Buddy makes it right."

Taryn Serwatowski is more than a fan. She is a disciple. She has loved Buddy Holly since the moment she heard his voice. "I was fifteen and sitting in my bedroom listening to the radio. 'That'll Be the Day' came on the air and it was love at first sound. I was hooked. In school I became known as 'The Buddy Holly Girl.' When I graduated from high school, I walked on stage to get my diploma and when my principal handed it to me and shook my hand, he screamed, 'Buddy Holly Lives!' Buddy changed my life."

Buddy is no passing phase for Taryn, who is now a graduate student at the University of Nebraska—Lincoln, where she is studying meteorology and climatology. Obviously very bright, Taryn teaches two undergraduate classes and carries a full load. After completing her graduate degree she says she will either apply for work with the Federal Aviation Administration or continue on to get her doctorate. And when studies become tough and times get hard? "I turn to Buddy."

In 1995, she explained, "my dad and I went on a Rock & Roll road trip. We left our home in Almont, Michigan, and drove to Lubbock to see

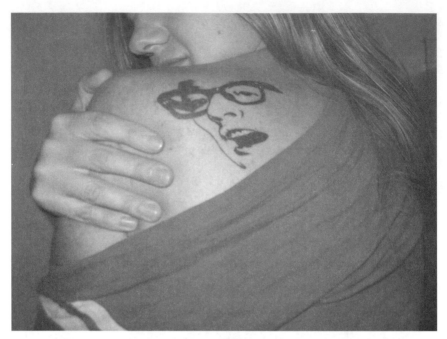

Taryn Serwatowski is more than just a Buddy Holly fan. She's a disciple. Buddy's music, she explains, "never fails to brighten my day." *Author*

all the Buddy sites, ending with the cemetery. It was an emotional event and a great father-daughter experience. My dad never criticized me for my love of Buddy. He embraced it."

"And I know you've heard John Mueller," I said.

"I am too young to have met Buddy, but I have met John Mueller. John's music is just like Buddy. When I first met John I was blown away by the resemblance. Being around John is the closest I'll come in this lifetime to being with Buddy."

"What is it about Buddy's music that keeps you coming back for more?" I asked.

"The sound of Buddy's music never fails to brighten my day," Taryn answers with a smile in her voice. "I have said that Buddy is always with me in my heart and mind, but 2010 was a difficult year for me, so I decided to make Buddy part of me in another way."

Taryn made a trip to a tattoo shop, where she asked to have Buddy's smiling face inked into her back and shoulder—almost full-size. Taryn can't seem to get Buddy out of her head and heart, and now she can't get him off her back!

"Buddy makes me feel unique and he is now part of my physical identity," she continued. "Buddy Holly is the true love of my life. I was just born too late."

Chapter 20

Will be the cure for me

Bill Griggs is arguably the world's leading Buddy Holly historian. "Bill," claims Jacqueline Bober, the curator at the Buddy Holly Center, "is our go-to guy for any information we need."

Bill is much more than a historian. He is a devoted fan and a Buddy apostle. His vocation is to keep Buddy's memory, history, and music alive. Bill grew up in Hartford, Connecticut, where he first heard the music that would change his life.

"Bill, how did you first become aware of Buddy Holly?" I asked.

"During the summer of 1957," he reminisced, when 'That'll Be the Day' by The Crickets came through my radio. It was love at first sound. I rushed to the record store to buy it. I'm a drummer and when I heard the tempo change, that impressed me. And the guitar, well, it was amazing."

In November of that year, the music came to Connecticut.

"Sixteen acts for ninety cents," Bill said. "Can you imagine that kind of value today? I went to see The Crickets and hear 'That'll Be The Day.' The Crickets came out second to last, and when they started playing 'Peggy Sue,' I looked at my friend Richard and said, 'The lead singer sounds just like that Buddy Holly guy!' 'He is!' Richard responded. 'He's the lead singer of The Crickets!' I had no idea they were one and the same. They were listed differently on record labels depending on the

Buddy Holly expert Bill Griggs (left), with author Gary Moore. *Author*

song, based upon contractual commitments, and the same was true of their listing on this tour."

The more Bill talked, the more excited he became. And he had used the phrase "love at first sound" to describe what he felt when he first heard Buddy's music—just like Taryn.

"These Rock & Roll shows back then were amazing! Like I said, ninety cents for sixteen acts and on top of it, the first two hundred people got a free record!" he exclaimed in a very excited voice. "The show was held at the State Theater. The State held 4,100 people and the house was packed!"

"Out of all those acts, why did Buddy stand out for you?" I asked.

"Buddy was different from the rest," replied Bill without missing a beat. "If you had a hit back then you would follow it up with a similar song in the same style. Not Buddy. He was too creative to do the same thing. He followed 'That'll Be The Day' with 'Peggy Sue' and then 'Oh Boy.' All were quite different from each other."

"So you were hooked," I responded with a chuckle.

"I stayed in for the second and third show that day at the State Theater! If we had walked out into the alley to the stage door between shows, I could have met Buddy! They were all there at a desk signing autographs," recalled Bill. "It is something I will always regret. I never got to meet him, but I witnessed a show that day that I'll never forget."

Fast forward to 1975.

"Buddy had been gone for sixteen years. I was disgusted that I was hearing nothing about him and could not find his records anywhere," Bill complained. "Buddy's songs were being covered extensively by others, but the Rock & Roll public had forgotten . . . or they were too young to know these songs were Buddy's? His own performances and recordings of his songs were pushed aside by the British Invasion and all the music that followed."

"The public in general has a short memory," I agreed.

"Yes. And in response to that fact, I started the Buddy Holly Memorial Society. We began with four hundred and nineteen members in the first year," said Bill. He was obviously proud of his accomplishment, as he should be. "It was so interesting. Fascinating, actually. People were joining from all over the world and they all expressed the same sentiment. Each person thought he or she was the last Buddy Holly fan on earth! Five years later the Buddy Holly Memorial Society had grown to five thousand and seven hundred members in thirty-four countries! This was all pre-Internet, of course, and pre-Buddy biographies."

"Did you ever hold a convention?" I asked.

"We sure did. Our first convention was in Connecticut. And we just kept growing," answered Bill. "The movie about Buddy Holly with Gary Busey, although totally inaccurate, showed people everywhere that there was this guy from Lubbock who wrote all the songs others were making careers upon. People learned that James Taylor didn't write 'Everyday,' that Linda Ronstadt wasn't the first to sing 'It's So Easy.' I think it really surprised a lot of people that 'Not Fade Away' was not by the Rolling Stones, and that 'Peggy Sue' was not by the Beach Boys. Buddy began making his comeback!"

"And you and your organization played a part in keeping the flame burning while waiting to reignite," I commented.

"Oh, I don't know what part I played, but Buddy began making his comeback," Bill modestly acknowledged. "The Crickets were one of the first self-contained bands," he continued. "They wrote, recorded, performed, and often produced their own material. I laugh when I hear people say The Beatles were the first to do that. Buddy did his own material and didn't cover others."

"And how did the Holley family respond to the Buddy Holly Memorial Society?" I asked.

"Buddy's mom, Mrs. Holley, attended several conventions. Our first was 1978. It was small but a beginning. But in 1980 we had more than eight hundred members attend our convention in Lubbock. They came from all over the world. We sat Mrs. Holley in a chair and introduced her to fans from England, Australia, Scotland, and Egypt," Bill paused and laughed.

Did I miss something? "What's so funny?" I asked.

"Mrs. Holley called me several days later and asked if all those people really came from all those places," chuckled Bill. "She was truly overwhelmed and touched. She had finally come to the realization that her son was actually famous in America, but she had no idea her Buddy was so loved, so admired and so adored around the globe." Bill paused. "I got great satisfaction in making that woman happy."

He continued. "In 1980, they dedicated the statue of Buddy in Lubbock and of course, I was there. As all the eyes were on the statue as they pulled the cover off, I was watching Mrs. Holley. The smile on her face made all the time and effort in preserving the history worth it. Buddy's mom's joy is what kept me going."

"Do you still have conventions?" I asked.

"No. When Mrs. Holley passed away we stopped the Buddy Holly Memorial Society, as it became too time-consuming and labor intensive. I couldn't take a vacation or any time off. Mrs. Holley was gone, and I thought it was the right time for me to move on," explained Bill.

"Mrs. Holley—I called her my surrogate grandma," he continued. "She would invite me over to just talk and usually not about Buddy. She just wanted the company. She was very religious, very polite. She never got over the death of her son. She realized that Buddy was not really appreciated in Lubbock because of the religious foundation of the community. 'Devil's Music'—that's what the paper called it," said Bill. "I think she appreciated my admiration and love for her son, and the fact I was working hard to capture and preserve his history and keep his memory alive. Back then I didn't realize what we were accomplishing. Photos were discovered and history was preserved. John Goldroscn, author of the Buddy bio *Remembering Buddy*, said the Buddy Holly Memorial Society became a clearing house for pictures and information. It was a valuable service, really," he said. "It happened and we didn't even realize it."

"So what happened after the end of the society?" I asked.

"I continued publishing the *Rockin-50s Magazine*. Fred Nock, my printer, went way above the call of duty to help restore photos that may have been unprintable," explained Bill. "We were in continuous publication for thirty years." I could detect the pride in his voice. "Now, I serve as an agent for many people who own Buddy photos, and I'm also an avid collector of all things Buddy, all while still running the www.rocking50s.com website."

"You did so much, Bill," I replied. "So what do you know about John Mueller?"

"John Mueller, Jay Richardson, and Ran Anthony are the best," Bill responded with enthusiasm. "I helped Jay really learn who his father was. Jay's mom did not share too much about his Big Bopper father until he was in his middle teens. I was able to fill in many blanks in reuniting Jay with his dad, who passed while his mom was pregnant with Jay. Things like this make me happy." Bill paused for a couple of seconds. "The thing with John Mueller is that he has a great resemblance to Buddy and cares about the music he performs, just as Buddy did. John is so much like Buddy in attitude, temperament, looks and sound. John is the best."

"John is who inspired my own journey," I replied.

"I could have started fan clubs for bigger names but I admired Buddy," continued Bill. "Elvis was enormously popular, but you know what the difference between Buddy and Elvis was?" he asked.

"What, Bill?"

"People came to see Elvis, but they came to hear Buddy."

I thought about it for a moment and realized how profound that statement was and, once again, it served as verification that Buddy was all about the music. "How did you end up moving from Connecticut to Lubbock?" I asked.

"I came to visit Lubbock and fell in love with West Texas," answered Bill. "I learned quickly that Buddy was molded and shaped by his surroundings. I call Buddy 'the gentleman of Rock & Roll.' He was always polite to his fans. You would rarely see him without a tie."

"And you attribute this to where he grew up?"

"I believe it was his West Texas upbringing that made him that way, yes I do," he answered strongly. "You cannot grow up in Texas and not be influenced. So I loved the attitude of the community and thought I'd try it for a year. I stayed. I love it here."

"You know so much about Buddy and have such a unique perspective, Bill," I said. "Tell me something else I don't know or need to know about Buddy."

"I believe Buddy's music is like Beethoven's. It will last forever." Bill's answer was delivered with firmness and clarity. There was no doubt in his mind. "The Rock & Roll of the fifties was special. It was fun. It was on the radio before Top Forty. You didn't care about the race or gender of the performers. No tattoos, no bare chests. Back then the artists cared about the music and not their image or shtick. For them," he added, "the money was a byproduct of the music. They did it for the love of the music."

"But you don't feel the same way about the music now?" I asked. "You feel very differently today."

"Rock & Roll died in '63 and became Rock," Bill replied.

"Can you tell me what you mean?" I asked.

"In the later '60s, Rock & Roll splintered. It became surf rock, psychedelic rock, protest rock, drug rock. It wasn't the fun Rock & Roll Buddy created. Buddy said, 'If we keep it simple, other people can play it.' It has mutated and become far from simple." Bill sighed heavily and stopped talking.

Bill Griggs has and continues to perform a valuable service for Buddy Holly. No one I know of has done as much to capture the history and preserve it for the ages. In recognition for this service, Bill was added to the West Texas Walk of Fame, where his name is permanently memorialized at the foot of the statue of the man Bill so admires. I know Buddy would be proud. When Bill was talking earlier, I found myself wishing he had stepped into that nameless alley and met Buddy in 1957 in Hartford, Connecticut. Buddy could not have known or even fully understood the role Bill would one day play in preserving his legacy, but it would have been a wonderful event in Bill's life.

Chapter 21

I'm gonna tell my blues

Human beings are attracted to tragedy. It's coded somewhere within our nature, buried deep within the recesses of our mind. In principle we say we would rather avoid the exposure, but as terrible events unfold we lock our eyes and hearts on to them and never let them go.

The Kennedy and Lincoln assassinations, the Battle of the Alamo, Custer's Last Stand, Pearl Harbor, the 9/11 attacks, the death of Marilyn Monroe and Princess Diana. Unexpected and tragic events involving premature death capture our minds and hearts as nothing else does. As they say in Sesser, Illinois, we are attracted to tragic events "like June bugs to a porch light." And yet, the very nature that attracts us to tragedy often encourages us to discount logic and fact and refuse to accept that something tragic happened as the facts suggest it did.

John F. Kennedy was killed by the CIA, the Mob or the Cubans (or all three!), 9/11 was an inside job perpetrated by our own government, Marilyn Monroe was killed at the direction of the Kennedy family, and Princess Diana was murdered by the Royals. Conspiracies develop quickly and take root in our culture. This is especially true when the death involves someone very famous or influential.

Former Tennessee Congressman David Crockett died at the Alamo at or before dawn on March 6, 1836. No credible historian doubts this and no evidence to the contrary exists. But for more than 50 years after his death many Americans, including politicians and Crockett family members, petitioned the Mexican government to release Crockett from the Mexico City dungeon where they believed he was being held. How could "Davy" Crockett, later dubbed by Walt Disney's marketing department as the "The King of the Wild Frontier," have been brought down even by thousands of Mexican soldiers? Something in our nature does not want to admit that heroes die, and they often die violently and too soon.

Buddy, Ritchie, the Big Bopper, and pilot Roger Peterson died on impact when the plane they were flying in hit the frozen ground of an Iowa farm field in February 1959. The Civil Aeronautics Board (CAB), the predecessor to the National Transportation Safety Board (NTSB) issued a straightforward report about what happened that night. Is there wiggle-room for discussion? Sure. It could have been ice developing on the surfaces of the leading edge of the wings and props that changed the aerodynamics of the plane and made it difficult to fly or completely unflyable. Most experts, however, do not think this is the case.

A detailed examination of the engine and plane demonstrated that everything was operating properly. It appears that the airplane was flown into the ground (not purposely, of course) in sound working order and between 165 and 170 mph. Some think that because of reduced visibility and no visible horizon, Roger Peterson suddenly found himself beyond his capabilities and was forced to rely upon his flight instruments. The young and largely inexperienced flyer (he was just 21 when he perished) thought he was climbing to a safe altitude when in fact he was initiating a very steep and sharp turn (more on that later) just feet off the ground. If he was misreading his instruments and initiated the turn (perhaps while trying to return to the Mason City airport), his wing dipped into the turn. The plane hit the frozen ground and cart-wheeled, throwing out the famous passengers against the frozen farm field. Professionals I spoke with agree there was no pain or suffering. Death was instantaneous for all aboard including the pilot, who remained trapped inside the wreckage.

I owned and operated both a flight school and an air charter service, and have spent many hours at the controls of both single and twin engine

Authorities study the wreckage on the morning of February 3, 1959. The plane came to rest against a barbed wire fence after rolling hundreds of feet over the frozen Iowa ground. Pilot Roger Peterson was still inside the cockpit. The passengers (Holly, Valens, and Richardson) had been thrown out. They died upon impact. *Globe Gazette*

aircraft while flying above farmland at night. Flying over flat farmland, with the absence of streetlights and other illumination to help orient you, creates a loss of reference and the lack of a horizon. In the best of cases, flying under these conditions is very difficult without the use of, experience with, and complete understanding of, the flight instruments in your panel. Wind gusts and snow only complicate matters. From Roger Peterson's perspective, looking out his windshield that night would have been much like entering warp speed with Han Solo in the Millennium Falcon—a dizzying blur of white specks racing out of the pitch black darkness and smashing into his windshield. The result for a young and inexperienced pilot would have been confusion and even vertigo.

Unfavorable weather and an inexperienced pilot is more than enough to create tragedy. Now add a high-performance aircraft (without de-icing abilities) like the V-Tail Bonanza into the mix. The Bonanza became known as the "Doctor and Lawyer Widow-maker" because professionals who did not fly for a living routinely purchased and died in this aircraft. Simply put, because of its high-performance level, in emergency situations it was difficult to manage.

Dwyer's Flying Service employed Roger Peterson, who was assigned to fly that night. The owner-operator of the charter service, Hubert J. "Jerry" Dwyer, was present at the airport as the plane was being loaded. He helped pack the luggage himself. Peterson, of course, could have refused to take off, but what young pilot would turn down the chance to fly three of the country's most popular Rock & Roll stars?

Jerry Dwyer was an experienced commercial pilot and his actions and presence that night at the airport encouraged Peterson to take off. As the owner of the charter service and of the plane itself, he could have refused to allow Peterson to take off. Obviously the young pilot demonstrated poor judgment that night, but Dwyer should not have put a

Another view of the demolished V-Tail Bonanza. *Globe Gazette*

young and inexperienced pilot in that plane in the middle of the night in the dead of winter with deteriorating weather conditions. According to the Civil Aeronautics Board report, those conditions were poor. Snow was falling, wind gusts were expected to be 30-50 knots along the flight path, and the visibility was decreasing. As the report concludes, "the decision to go was *most imprudent* [emphasis added]." The plane took off at 12:55 a.m. on February 3. Dwyer remained on the platform outside the tower to watch. According to the report, "When about five miles from the airport, Dwyer watched the tail light of the aircraft gradually descend until it was out of sight." Something nagged at me as I read these words. It was the middle of winter and freezing cold. Why did Dwyer stand outside for five long minutes to watch his pilot take off? Why did he go with his pilot to check weather conditions? Pilots routinely do this sort of thing, and they do this *alone*. I know because I owned a charter service. Given the details revealed in the report, the answer seems obvious: given the deteriorating weather conditions Dwyer did not trust the pilot, and he was worried about the flight from the very beginning.

What also seems obvious is that if you put an inexperienced pilot behind the controls of a high-performance plane in the dead of night with bad weather, bad things can happen. And in this case, the worst thing that could have happened did happen. So how do conspiracies bloom out of something so apparent?

When I owned the flight school and air charter service in Kankakee, my chief pilot and flight instructor was a wonderful young man, dear friend, and outstanding pilot named Roberto Martinez (who we affectionately called Robert-O). As I mentioned earlier, we made a refueling stop at the Mason City Airport in the early 1990s, and the young man who helped us commented that the Holly plane wreckage was hidden away in one of the hangers. After we took off, Robert-O said, "You know, that pilot flew his plane right into the ground."

"Why would he do that?" I asked, although I was not even sure what pilot and what plane he was talking about.

"Who knows," he answered casually and with a shrug, "but the rumor is that there was a bullet hole in the back of the pilot's seat."

"The shape of the mass of wreckage approximated a ball with one wing sticking up from the mass diagonally from one side." — Cerro Gordo County's Coroner's Investigation Report. *Globe Gazette*

"What?" I asked. A bullet hole? Only then did I realize he was talking about the Holly crash, although I barely knew who Buddy Holly was at the time. "The pilot was shot in the back?"

"That's what they say," replied Robert-O.

"They? Who is they?" I asked. "The NTSB?"

"I don't know," he answered. "But it's widely known and discussed in aviation circles." I didn't know anything about the crash, and had no reason to believe that what Robert-O was telling me wasn't accurate.

How does a rumor like this become widely discussed and circulated? In this case it was because the authorities found a gun at the crash site—and it was later determined to have belonged to Buddy. That is a verifiable fact. When I heard that, my response was immediate: "So what? Buddy was a Texan. It was legal and it was his constitutional right to own a gun."

So how does owning and possessing a gun morph into shooting the pilot—and why would he? Was Buddy suicidal? Was he mentally unstable? Did the pilot offend Buddy to the point that Buddy wanted to shoot him? If so, the argument was a very brief one—a few minutes at most before they took off. The pilot was almost certainly wearing headphones and trying to deal with bad weather. He would not have heard any comments made in the noisy plane, so I can't even imagine a plausible scenario regarding a dispute with the pilot during the flight.

For argument's sake, if there was some heated dispute we have to believe Buddy was willing to shoot the pilot—the only man qualified to fly the plane—with the certainty that it would also end his own life and the lives of everyone else aboard. No one has ever suggested or even insinuated that Buddy was suicidal or mentally unstable, and nothing in his personal or professional life even hinted as much. And there is no documented account of any animosity or issues between him and his fellow performers who flew on the plane that night.

According to the Cerro Gordo County's Coroner's Investigation Report, all three passengers had been thrown from the plane upon impact. Buddy Holly's remains are visible on the left. Richie Valens' body is on the right. Jay "Big Bopper" Richardson was thrown into the field beyond, and is not visible in this photo. *Globe Gazette*

The first person to approach the plane was County Sheriff Bill McGill about 9:35 a.m. Jerry Dwyer, the plane's owner, had discovered the wreckage about thirty minutes earlier during an aerial search. *Globe Gazette*

Someone suggested to me that Buddy might have been cleaning the gun and that it accidentally discharged during flight. Anyone who thinks that is possible has never sat in the cramped cockpit of a Beechcraft Bonanza. There's very little room to do anything but sit and go along for the ride. Also, it was very dark that night. There was no light in the cockpit other than from the instrumentation, and the pilot would not have turned on any light because it would have affected his night vision. Based on all the facts as I know them, there was also a fair amount of turbulence. No one was cleaning anything on that short plane ride.

I heard a new conspiracy theory today, a variation and expansion on the rumor that Buddy shot the pilot. Someone on Facebook informed me that after the plane crashed, Buddy and the Big Bopper survived. The Big Bopper tried to crawl to a farm house for help, and that was when Buddy finished him off with the handgun by shooting him in the back. Afterward, Buddy died from his crash injuries. Is it possible to suggest something more absurd? But, I checked anyway. No, the Big Bopper did not have a bullet hole anywhere in his body, and he was in no shape to

GLOBE GAZETTE

The coroner arrived at the scene about 11:15 a.m. By that time, members of the Highway Patrol, local media, and "spectators" were also examining the wreckage. *Globe Gazette*

crawl anywhere. Buddy and J. P. Richardson died on impact with Ritchie and Roger.

I suppose it is possible that the gun discharged accidentally. Does the coroner's report provide any clues to support this theory? As a matter of fact it does by what it does not say. Nowhere does the report mention a bullet in pilot Roger Peterson or anyone else. Nor is there any mention of a bullet hole in Buddy's overnight bag, in which the gun was carried. The gun broke through the bottom of the bag on impact and did not discharge. Bill Griggs, perhaps the world's leading authority on Buddy, owns the overnight bag. According to Bill, it does not have a bullet hole. The talk about gunfire in the airplane is nonsense.

There is more solid evidence dispelling this myth. In the spring of 1959, a farmer with the last name of Juhl rented the field where the plane went down. He was plowing months after the crash debris had been removed when he found the handgun. He climbed off his tractor and picked it up. To Juhl's surprise, when he lifted the barrel toward the sky and pulled the trigger, the gun discharged. He took the gun to the county

A member of the Highway Patrol examines some of the wreckage. He and other investigators approached the downed plane in a circuitous route to avoid disturbing the debris field, which stretched for 570 feet. *Globe Gazette*

sheriff, whose examination revealed that it had only one spent cartridge. The handgun had been fired one time and the farmer was the man who shot it. This fact, coupled with the lack of a bullet hole in the pilot, is conclusive proof that Buddy's gun had nothing to do with the crash of the Bonanza.

Why can't conspiracy theorists just accept the fact that the combination of deteriorating weather conditions, low visibility at night, a high-performance aircraft, and an inexperienced pilot at the controls combined into a deadly recipe?

Chapter 22

Don't come back Knockin

"The truth has never been told about what happened on that flight."

Barb Dwyer's words still echo in my head. What is the truth? She wasn't on the plane and neither was her husband Jerry. Do they know more than the investigators? Do they have information about the flight they have never revealed? If so, why would they wait more than fifty years and still refuse to reveal it? My gut and my brain tell me the Dwyers are two good people in the twilight of their lives who still feel the need to defend themselves for Jerry's decision to let that flight leave the ground. As a former charter operator, I understand how he must feel. The weight of that decision must be a heavy burden to carry, and he carries it each and every day.

The deaths of Buddy, Ritchie, and the Big Bopper continue to intrigue people, as they have intrigued me. I didn't believe for a moment that a gunshot or some struggle aboard the plane caused the crash, but as a pilot I was curious about exactly what did happen early that morning in February 1959. I decided to do something about it.

I contacted the National Transportation Safety Board (NTSB), and someone I spoke with was kind enough to put me in touch with Dick Rodriguez, an experienced and seasoned accident investigator now retired and residing in Florida. He had an interest in the crash, and agreed

The point of impact. One of the plane's wings struck the ground here at 165-170 miles per hour before tumbling nearly 600 feet. It came to rest against a barbed wire fence and post. *Globe Gazette*

to read the entire report. Dick and I discussed the report and various issues relating to the crash via telephone on two different occasions. Both conversations were long and substantive.

"A couple of things jump out at me," Dick said during one of our conversations. "The report states that the needles on the instruments were frozen. Usually a high impact crash like this will find the needles broken off. The fact that these are intact, gives us a look inside the cockpit at the moment of impact," Dick explained from his Pensacola home. "The rate of climb indicator indicates the plane struck the ground while descending at 3,000 feet per minute. That is a very high rate of descent. I don't think it was strictly a matter of misreading the instruments, but more likely that the aircraft became upset by its natural tendency to roll into a bank, which can develop rapidly into a graveyard spiral from which Peterson was too inexperienced to recover using only his instruments."

"Upset by its natural tendency to roll into a bank?" I repeated his statement back to him as a question.

"Yes. I've called several friends who have logged hours in a Bonanza," continued Dick. "They say the plane is not unusually unstable or unforgiving, but once upset with little or no visibility and established in a spiral, you have to be an extremely skilled pilot to recover using instruments only. That is true of any airplane."

"And this was a pitch dark night without a visible horizon," I added.

"In the brightness of day and with clear weather it may have been a different story," admitted Dick, "but when the aircraft is upset and you have no visual reference point outside the plane, you must recover by interpreting your instruments and reacting accordingly. This young man didn't even have an instrument rating, and when he had previously taken his instrument flight test, he failed." Dick paused before adding, "I wouldn't like his odds of recovering."

Roger Peterson, the pilot Jerry Dwyer hired to fly three of the biggest musical names in America, had failed his instrument flight test.

"So take me through the scenario that most likely took place," I asked the aviation accident expert. "How do you think this plane came to be in this fatal circumstance?"

"Okay," Dick begins. "According to the report, the pilot said he would file his flight plan en route. There are reasons pilots do this, usually in high traffic areas, but I'm not sure any of these reasons existed in Mason City, Iowa, after midnight. Regardless, Dwyer let him take off knowing the flight plan had not been filed. So the plane rolls down the runway, becomes airborne and is off to Fargo. The pilot was then expected to contact Mason City to file his plan, which he was probably reviewing.

"There was turbulence in the area," continued Dick, "and I believe he was most likely feeling it. While focused on his preparation to file, the plane likely rolls to the right, whether a function of turbulence or natural roll, the nose naturally lowers, which easily can happen without warning. By the time Peterson recognizes the upset condition of the aircraft, the attitude had reached the point beyond his skill level to recover."

"What do you think he did then?" I asked, even though as a former pilot I had a good idea of the answer.

"With no visual reference to assist recovery, the natural reaction of most pilots is to pull back on the yoke to remain airborne," explained Dick, "but in this case, it only increases the rate of turn and becomes unrecoverable. Had there been a visual horizon, he could have possibly leveled his wings and recovered."

While Dick was painting a vivid picture of what likely took place inside the cockpit, I began to imagine the panic that must have coursed through the cabin. I was in a Cessna 152 during my flight training and purposefully stalled the plane on several occasions. Recovery is easy—if you recognize what is happening.

On one of my early flight lessons the instructor purposely stalled the plane. My immediate reaction was the result of years of driving a car: I stepped hard on my left rudder as if it were a car brake. This action rolled the plane over into the beginning of a spiral. I can honestly admit this began the most frightening few seconds of my entire life. My flight instructor knew what to do, of course, and quickly reacted to recover control and resume stable flight. But in the dark of night without reference points it is difficult to recognize up from down and left from right. Vertigo sets in and the ground comes quickly. In order to recover, you have to know what direction you are spinning and the difference between up and down. At night, with no visible horizon or point of reference, an inexperienced pilot will have trouble properly interpreting the situation and reacting appropriately.

"Dick, is there anything else that could have happened?" I asked.

"Sure," he replied. "Unless you were there, you never know, but I have seen similar cases over and over through the years."

"I guess the 3,000 feet per minute rate of descent is a big clue."

"Yes it is," Dick replied, "and so is the way that plane struck the ground—wing first, in a 90-degree turn (wings perpendicular to the ground) and nose down attitude at that high rate of speed really paints the vivid picture of a spiral," Dick concluded.

Those words, spoken by an aviation crash expert, chilled me. There was no sudden accident, as we had been led to believe for so long. Those young men aboard that doomed plane knew they were in trouble long before they hit the ground.

Chapter 23

Cause I'm changin all those changes

Where is it?

Jerry Dwyer has been telling locals and many people who have inquired over the ensuing decades that he has the plane. He claimed he buried the wreckage at an undisclosed location and will dig it up as a life insurance policy in the future. Remember the lineman back in the early 1990s who had pointed to a hanger and claimed he had been told the plane wreckage was hidden inside?

If Dwyer really has it, why is he hiding it? If there is a bullet hole in the pilot's seat—or in any other part of the instrumentation or fuselage—it might explain something other than what the CAB reported. However, we know with certainty there was no bullet in Peterson's body, and a bullet lodged in the seat would not have caused the plane to become unstable. And, of course, the authorities have accounted for all the bullets in Buddy Holly's gun: the farmer discharged one round and the rest were still in the gun.

Barb Dwyer told me Jerry was writing a book about the entire episode and that "the truth" will finally be told. But neither Barb nor Jerry was in the plane and no one witnessed the crash, so what could they possibly know that no one else does? Does the wreckage hold some undisclosed or undiscovered evidence? I doubt it, and so does retired NTSB aviation expert Dick Rodriquez, but on what other basis could Barb Dwyer make such a claim?

I was not going to address the plane crash in any meaningful way when I began writing this book. My intention when I phoned the Dwyers was simply to interview them like I did everyone else. Like it or not, their lives were impacted by Buddy Holly. Unfortunately, it was in a very negative way. I respect the Dwyers, their advancing age, and appreciate the heartache they must have suffered, but I cannot write *Hey Buddy* and ignore Barb Dwyer's bold claim, repeated several times, that they know something about the crash that know one else does—"the truth."

If the Dwyers are really holding the plane, perhaps it is because they believe the wreckage has evidence that clears Jerry's conscience for letting the flight leave on that fateful early morning. If so, then maybe he has not released this evidence or let others see the plane because he is waiting to finish and release his book. But if the wreckage held some lost secret that cleared his conscience (and would stun the world, as it most surely would), why would the Dwyers wait more than five decades to release it?

If Jerry Dwyer really has the plane wreckage, the emotional value to Buddy, Ritchie, and Big Bopper enthusiasts worldwide would be off the charts. Given how well known its occupants were and the fatal event, the wreckage could be worth a fortune to the Dwyers. Why not unveil it or sell it? I am not suggesting they should benefit financially, but why continue to hide it if you have it—especially if it supports Barb's statement that only they know "the truth" about what happened that night?

If they really have the plane, let us see it. If the pilot seat has a bullet hole, show us. If the plane somehow tells a different story of the events of that night than do the official documents, let the plane speak the truth that Barb insists only they know. If Dick Rodriguez (like the CAB before him) is wrong, let the plane tell the story or share with the world facts heretofore unrevealed. If the wreckage is available, experts using today's higher level of technology should be allowed to examine it once again. I would help pull together a team of qualified and unbiased experts who can support or dispel this untold "truth." Both the CAB and now NTSB have a well known and longstanding policy that no investigation is ever closed. The NTSB is always open to receiving new and pertinent evidence on any accident investigation.

Is it even possible that the Dwyers have the plane wreckage? Dick Rodriguez and I discussed this very issue in one of our conversations. In most cases when a plane is totaled, he explained, one of the conditions of the insurance carrier is that the carrier gets the wreckage in exchange for payment.

Was that the case here? If so, did Jerry Dwyer forgo payment for the plane in order to bury or hide it? That seems highly doubtful.

According to Buddy Holly expert Bill Griggs, he ran into the same roadblocks I did trying to get through to the Dwyers. Close friends of the Dwyers told Bill that Jerry purchased the plane for salvage and that they have seen the wreckage. Apparently Jerry has the instruments from the wrecked plane and has showed them to people. When I asked Bill whether he knew for certain that those instruments were from the downed plane or from another Bonanza, Bill admitted he had no idea other than what others had related. Perhaps the Dwyers did purchase the plane as salvage from the insurance carrier. Bill is confident that they did, and he is equally confident that the Dwyers still have the wreckage.

If so, why go to all that trouble and expense to buy the plane, just to hide it for decades?

This is easy to settle: Jerry, you should show the world the plane.

Put unfounded rumors to bed, once and for all. The NTSB is open to any new information you may have that would change their original findings. I know because I have asked them.

**If you do not have the plane, please issue
a statement and put an end to the speculation.**

Regardless of where the wreckage is or isn't, please tell us what you know. Tell us your *truth*.

Let me put it another way:

Jerry,

I will assemble a team of first class aviation experts to examine the wreckage you claim to have in your possession to help you substantiate the reasons for the crash. If the "truth" has never been told, let me help you tell it. If the CAB report is correct, let us help verify that fact so we can put all the conspiracies and doubts to rest. But if one of those conspiracies (or something else entirely) turns out to be true, let the truth be told! Jerry, you are the only man in the world who can either help make this happen or forever block the truth from being told. Will you join with me and allow the world to know what actually happened

Gary

*   *   *

The Dwyers are fine people. I talked to several locals off the record who know them and everyone attests to that fact. The accident on February 3, 1959, was exactly that—an accident. If he could do it all over again, Jerry Dwyer would never have let that plane take off.

*   *   *

It is human nature to seek a larger or more noble or interesting reason for a tragedy to measure up to the importance of the people who die before their time. Ritchie Valens, J. P. "Big Bopper" Richardson, and Buddy Holly died in the prime of their young and promising lives because of a decision by an air charter operator to let a V-Tail Bonanza aircraft take off in bad weather with a young and inexperienced pilot at the controls who was not instrument rated. The results were not *expected*, but they were *foreseeable*.

Our hearts cry out for more, where more does not exist. Sometimes in life, it simply is what it is.

Chapter 24

And I'll be a rocking

"Okay, here is what you need to know. I'm not a Rock & Roll expert, but compared to you, I'm a world-renowned authority," laughed Tim Duggan.

"Yeah, I get it. Just tell me the basics and where I should begin," I replied. I was smiling as well because we both knew he was right.

"I've burned some CDs for you."

"Of what?"

"Of my favorite songs and artists. I'm a fan," Tim explained. "Like most people, my musical tastes revolve around the sounds and artists I listened to between the ages of twelve and twenty-four. Yeah, I like some of the new stuff, but the golden era for me was in my formative years. My bet is that is true for most people, but that's just my opinion."

"That makes sense to me," I said as I reached for the stack of CDs in Tim's hand.

"Not so fast," he responded, pulling the CDs back from my grasp. "You need some quick instruction."

"Instruction? I know how to listen to music!"

"Apparently not or we wouldn't be having this conversation." Score one for Tim. "I do have to ask you a question first."

"Shoot."

"Please tell me you know who the Beatles are and what they mean to music and culture in general."

I rolled my eyes. "I know the Beatles," I assured him.

"Good. Then we can start with my favorite group, The Who," said Tim.

"Who?" I asked.

"The Who," Tim repeated.

"Sounds like the beginning of an Abbot and Costello skit," I said.

"Are you going to take this seriously?" Tim asked sharply. "I don't want to waste my time."

"Yes, of course."

"The Who is different than all the other bands of our generation," Tim began.

"How?" I asked.

"The standard of the time was a lead guitar, rhythm guitar, bass guitar, and drums," he explained with more patience than I deserved. "In every case the drums, bass, and rhythm guitar were strictly support for the vocals, while the lead guitar added a little extra."

"You just described the Crickets, at least at one point in time," I pointed out. "There were also times where they were a trio with one guitar only."

"Really?" asked Tim. "The early Beatles were a typical foursome, but I think you are right. This configuration may have begun with the Crickets and inspired The Beatles and almost every other early Rock combo," Tim acknowledged. "But not The Who. With The Who, every instrument is the lead and all four instruments play lead at the same time! You can tune into each and every instrument and it is playing its own counterpoint to the lead. Even the drums."

"Sounds like a mess."

He shook his head. "Listen to this CD first, Gary. There is not a nanosecond of mess. Only incredibly creative and complex music. I believe listening to The Who raises your I.Q." Tim handed me the CD and smiled. "So . . . you really need this."

"Nice," I responded.

Tim was really into this. He was excited about sharing his knowledge and love of his music. He continued with enthusiasm, lifting up a second CD. "This is 'The Boss,' Bruce Springsteen. Bruce plays blue collar, hard working Rock & Roll." Tim held out the CD but I didn't reach for it.

"What?" Tim asked.

"I'm not excited about his politics," I said.

Tim tossed the CD into my lap. "Get over it. We're talking music here, not the state of the Union. Bruce and his E Street Band always figure prominently into any discussion of American rock & roll. We can't have this discussion without talking about The Boss."

"Okay. What else?"

"Led Zeppelin," Tim said, handing me another CD.

"This is 'Stairway to Heaven,' right?" I said.

"Impressive," Tim responded with surprise. "How do you know Stairway?"

"I've seen Wayne's World." I handed the Led Zeppelin CD back to Tim, who leaned over to reach for it. Just as he was about to take it, I pulled it back and in my best Mike Myers impersonation said, "Stairway denied!"

"You are so goofy," Tim said, shaking his head while trying his best to hide a smile. "You really are, you know."

"Is that it?" I asked.

"Well, The Doors, of course, but you need to talk to your buddy Jim Riordan about them. He literally and figuratively wrote the book on Jim Morrison, so see him for the details. He'll tell you what you need to know, but they were different. Their music didn't sound like anyone before or since. I think as part of your Buddy Holly project, they may not really fit. You can find a little Buddy in The Who, The Boss, Led Zeppelin and almost every early Rock band, but I can't hear anything but pure Doors in Doors music."

"Okay. Well, I'll skip The Doors and leave them for another day. What else?"

"That's more than you need to begin. I think this is a great start and introduction to all of the music you foolishly missed."

"Is there anything in particular I should listen for?" I asked.

Tim Duggan, my long-time friend and business associate who is also a self-styled Rock music instructor and philosopher. *Tim Duggan*

Tim thought for a moment and then continued. "The one thing that strikes me is that from Buddy forward, the music evolved steadily but the lyrics made a quantum leap in direction," he explained. "Buddy, early Beatles, and really all the music of the fifties and early sixties is about love, teenage crushes, holding hands, and the girl next door. You didn't hear much if any overt sex, violence, or drugs. Then it changed." Tim paused again.

"How so?" I asked.

"The lyrics—their intensity. They start becoming angry and focused on social issues, the generation gap, and Vietnam," Tim continued. "The divide between the World War II generation and the Baby Boomers became pronounced in the lyrics of the music of the late sixties. A female friend of mine refers to The Who as 'angry male music,' and I think it's a good description."

"Okay," I said slowly. "And how do you think all this relates to Buddy?"

"The music is all part of the natural Buddy lineage," Tim answered confidently, "but the topics and lyrics are not. Does that make sense? Buddy's lyrics are more in tune with the decade of the fifties." Tim looked at me, his eyebrows arched high as he waited to see my reaction.

I understood exactly what he meant. "Maybe that's why Buddy almost seemed to disappear during the sixties and seventies, but seems to have come roaring back as the anger of that generation subsided," I wondered aloud. "So do you think the lyrics are a reflection of the mood of the generation, or did the lyrics incite the mood?"

"Probably a little of both," said Tim. "Teenagers were becoming heard and seen. In the fifties and before that time, kids really didn't have a voice in adult affairs. Think about it. The young artists of the sixties gave their generation a new vehicle to express their opinions and even to take a stance on a big event of the day. Can you think of a time before that when teenagers would dare participate in the national dialogue, much less try to direct it?" asked Tim. I shook my head as he continued. "This change was both rapid and radical, like many of the changes during this time. So I guess it was a reflection of the new generation's aspirations, but also a call to arms that swelled the ranks of the young who became politically and socially active."

"I get that," I assured him. "But I had teenagers and you have teenagers now. Do you want them setting the political and social agenda for the future?"

"No, of course not," he firmly replied, "but the question and my answer are irrelevant. Go back to the early sixties with me. It has nothing to do with their maturity level. The music was being made by kids their own age and they were demanding input into these social and political issues. It was the arrogance of youth that demanded a say in national or world affairs—a role in political and social structures and even equality (or at least respect) within their own family units. The music was played and created by their peers for them."

"Give me a song that you think represents that," I said.

"Sure—'My Generation' by The Who from 1965." Tim replied. "Musically it's unique because it's the first song to feature a solo rift from the bass player. More importantly it is a radical call to action to the post

World Word II generation. It says 'I hope I die before I get old.' Writer Pete Townshend is taking a blatant stab at his parents' generation by declaring that his generation has its own values and vision of how the world should be. If getting older leads to losing youthful idealism and passion, then it would be better to die before that happens. By 'old' he is speaking of a state of mind, not an age," he added.

"So 'My Generation' is a rejection of the values of his parents' generation?"

Tim nodded and continued. "More importantly, it is a demand to be heard and treated equally. It's not personally aimed at Mom and Dad individually, but it is squarely aimed at Mom and Dad's generation as a whole. Roger Daltrey sings the words with passion and without compromise. Again, the arrogance of youth." Tim smiles. "I just love The Who."

"And that is where it all loses me," I sighed. "I remember our young men and women in uniform being spat upon. I remember the SDS and the Weather Underground blowing up the Haymarket Square Statue in Chicago and the Pentagon. I remember Abbie Hoffman, wrapped in the American Flag he despised, screaming on TV. I only see him as a criminal. You and Jim Riordan talk about it all in glowing terms, while I find it shameful. Was that all incited by the music?"

"No," Tim answered quickly. "Well . . . yes." Tim struggled to get his footing here. "Well, some of it. But first of all, I'm not glowing. Some of what happened is shameful, but much of it was not. The point, Gary, is that all that stuff is irrelevant to this conversation. I thought you wanted to talk about the music. You keep trying to force a political or social discussion. You've jumped the track. Let me be clear. I think you are talking about a narrow bandwidth of the music led by Bob Dylan and the anti-war movement. I'm not talking about the politics at all. I'm trying to introduce you to the music and the voice our generation was finding on all sorts of subjects." Tim paused and his eyes narrowed. "So what is pulling you elsewhere?"

"I don't know," I reply with a shrug as I brush off his question. Deep inside, though, I really did know. A memory from my past was surfacing. I see a friend of mine, a young teenage girl carrying an American flag down the street, crying. For years I have been lumping the music and the actions I detested by of some members of my generation into the same pile. Intellectually I understood the difference, but emotionally I had not separated the two. Hey, Buddy. I didn't expect you to bring me here.

"The more you talk, the more I realize you would be an admirer of The Who's Pete Townshend," Tim said.

I barely heard Tim because I was lost in my emerging epiphany. How did I travel from John Mueller's Winter Dance Party in February to this point? Where had I been all the years before?

Tim could see my mind was drifting in another direction. "Hey! Stay with me here!" he demanded. "When Abbie Hoffman jumped onto the stage at Woodstock to make a speech, Pete hit him in the head with his guitar, knocking him off the stage, then told the crowd that 'The next f—-ing person who walks across this stage is going to get f—-ing killed.' You see, while a few had a specific anti-war agenda, it wasn't about the politics for Pete and most of the sixties musicians. It's all about the music. You're stuck on Abbie Hoffman, who probably couldn't carry a tune," laughed Tim. I was staring down at the CDs I was holding and didn't offer a reply. "You know what I think Buddy would say?" Tim asked. When I didn't respond he answered his own question: "It's all about the music."

Chapter 25

Hey, Buddy rave on

"Never before in history has a generation been so focused on doing such great things and had so few resources to pull them off," Jim Riordan began. Jim, of course, is the bestselling author of *Break on Through*, the definitive biography of Jim Morrison. It seemed like a good idea to speak with him again after my conversation with Tim Duggan. "We just didn't have the connections, money, and power to make it happen."

"Make what happen, Jim?" I asked

"Peace," Jim responded.

"Peace? You were trying to make peace?" I asked.

"Yes."

"By trying to blow up the Pentagon? By blowing up the Haymarket Square statue in Chicago? Blowing things up creates peace?" Jim looked at me as I continued. "Calling police officers who risk their lives to protect us 'pigs'? Spitting at soldiers who were only doing their duty? This was all to bring peace? I'm not buying it."

He sighed. "Well, no. Not when you put it that way." Jim paused. "It was a strange time, man. Like most movements that start for the right reasons, the power can get into the wrong hands and the focus can be lost."

"It was a strange time. I really don't know how history will judge our generation," I said with concern.

Jim looked puzzled. "What do you mean?"

"With the benefit of time, cause and effect becomes more apparent. With every passing day, our parents become more clearly part of what Tom Brokaw dubbed 'The Greatest Generation,' and I believe they were. They answered the call of duty. They didn't protest or burn their draft cards. There were no American flags burning in the streets. They weren't running to Canada. They stood up, answered the call and saved the free world as we know it. But not just the men. The women did their part, too. My mom was sixteen when she was welder in the Oakland shipyards. The kids were out collecting scrap metal. Our parent's generation pulled together for a common cause unlike any generation in history," I continued. "They were far from perfect, but their sacrifice has given us so much of what our generation and the rest of the world has enjoyed."

"Our generation also pulled together for a common cause. Our cause was different. Their war was a different war," explained Jim.

"Yes, it was," I answered, nodding in agreement. "I understand and accept that, but the contrasts between attitudes, willingness to work for the common good, and a love of country are stark. Our parents' generation went to war, saved the free world, and came home to build the greatest nation in history and never complained about doing it. And that was after growing up in the Great Depression with nothing!"

"Yeah, I'll give you that," shot back Jim. "But our parents never felt lied to and deceived by their government." He raised his voice a notch. "LBJ [President Lyndon B. Johnson] lied about all of it. When the vets started coming home, they verified that the war was not what was being presented at home."

"I think you are talking about a small minority of vets," I replied. "John Kerry is not representative of the majority of veterans."

Jim sat back and smiled as he ran his fingers through his white hair. "What's gotten into you?"

"Buddy."

He nodded as if he already knew the answer. "Cool. So your discovery of Buddy Holly is leading you to the next step, and you want to know more about the larger cultural picture. That's cool, man. It really is."

"Buddy was a pioneer of the music and culture of our generation. Do you agree with that?" I asked.

"Like I told you the last time we talked, Buddy was just a couple years before my time," Jim answered. "I began engaging with music when I was about twelve or thirteen or so. Buddy died when I was just nine."

"Set Buddy aside for a moment. Give me your best shot. Tell me why I should not be ashamed and embarrassed by the actions of my generation." I sat back to hear Jim answer.

"Why?"

"Because I'm beginning to understand that I am tying the music of the time to events that may not be related. I would really like to disconnect them if I can, but I need to know more and understand what happened."

"I don't get it." Jim shook his head.

"Humor me on this one," I pleaded. "Give me your best shot. I don't know who else could explain it better."

"Okay," Jim began, looking down to the side for a moment as if to collect his thoughts. "It's like this. Our intentions were honest. Our mission was pure. We believed we could all live together on this planet in peace and harmony. We were at Woodstock without violence. We believed we could expand the message from there. But it all got away from us. Splinter groups started believing we could levitate the Pentagon by meditating. Free love led to STDs and recreational drugs led to addiction and violence. The sentiments are still correct," he hastened to add. "The ideas are still good! We just didn't have the power to pull it off."

"Levitate the Pentagon?" I laughed.

Jim shrugged. "There's more to it. I now also realize that the movement was not grounded in faith. I think what was missing from this generation was Jesus. We were grounded to nothing but our ideals and they were floating around with nothing to anchor them on," Jim said with real resignation in his voice.

"You know, Jim, by all accounts Buddy Holly was a man of deep faith. He used his first royalty check to buy new pews for his church, and Buddy and his partner-producer Norman Petty both tithed," I said. "The more I learn about him the more examples I discover of Buddy living his life as a witness of his faith, rather then being vocal and up front about it. His actions and interactions with others reveal a kind, loving, respectful, and faithful young man."

"Interesting." Jim seemed genuinely surprised by this news about Buddy. "Compare that to The Beatles and the Stones. They were searching for religion elsewhere but had no faith and no grounding. When you are unanchored, you are but a lost ship at sea, man."

Levi Storm. Something about the 1960s still lingers—don't you think? *Jim Riordan*

"You think they were lost?" I asked.

"Yes," Jim answered.

"I agree," I answered. "And The Beatles and Stones were driving the culture in the 60s. They followed Buddy's lead musically. Would he have impacted them spiritually? If Buddy had lived, would he have made a difference?"

Jim furrowed his brow and pursed his lips. We both sat lost in our thoughts imagining the "what ifs." I broke the silence. "Let's get back to the details."

"Let's go back to that whole thing about the violence," Jim continued. "They were against Martin Luther King until the Black Panthers emerged, then King looked good to the establishment."

"They?" I asked. "They who?"

"The establishment, man. Those with and in control." Jim looked at me as if I clearly should have known the "they" he was talking about.

I smiled. "You really mean 'the man,' right?"

Jim laughed but ignored my prodding. "The same may be true of the hippies. We started looking mainstream when the Weather Underground started blowing things up. Now just to be clear, I'm not condoning violence or what they did. I'm just stating the facts." Jim's head was tilted forward and his eyes were looking straight at me with the most serious professorial gaze he could muster. "The violent actions of the few—and I emphasize 'few', brought the establishment into a position to accept the mainstream peace movement."

"OK, let's say I agree," I replied. "What did you accomplish?"

"The Vietnam War ended. If not for the protests, how long would it have gone on?" There was that look again.

I shook my head. "I don't know, of course, but some historians make a pretty good case that the social unrest at home lengthened the war. They think the social unrest and growing protests prevented the government from allowing the military to fight to win." I paused for a moment before asking, "Do you believe that?"

"I don't know," Jim sighed. "To win what exactly? I just don't know a single person who really has a clue about what we were doing there in the first place!"

"Let me take you back to the music. Was it a reflection of the times or did it drive the times?" I asked.

"Both. How do you separate the two?" asked Jim. "The musicians were giving us a voice. They were encouraging action and empowering the youth. It all started with the Beatles. They were our age or just a little older—members of our own generation. They had the microphone and their words resonated with the masses of their peers and —."

"What about Buddy?" I interjected. "The Beatles claim that Buddy was their mentor and their model. Their early music reflected the same sentiments and ideals. If Buddy had lived, would the direction of the country have changed? Would the sixties have been a different decade?"

Jim shook his head. "Not unless Buddy could have prevented or stopped the war. The 60s as we know it was because of, and driven by, the war in Vietnam and the government's misinformation and lies. How could Buddy have stopped that? And The Beatles did not start it. They began in the same spirit as Buddy but the times and events changed them. Why wouldn't the same forces have changed Buddy?"

"Because of Buddy's faith?" I asked. "Didn't you say that part of the failure of the peace movement was the lack of an anchor?"

"Hmm . . . right," he replied. "The ideals floated and evolved because they were not tethered."

"The lack of faith within the movement? Jesus?" I asked more as a rhetorical question than anything else. "Buddy was anchored. He only lost the microphone as a result of his death. Would things have been different if he had the microphone in the 60s?"

"You're really into this," Jim said. "This Buddy thing is really pushing your buttons. This isn't like you." He paused. "Why?"

I shrugged and looked down at the open palms of my hands.

Chapter 26

And sing us a song

Buddy died eleven months before the sixties began, but he helped lay the foundation upon which the music of the 1960s was built. I was more deeply impacted by the events of my generation than I had realized or wanted to admit. Tim Duggan's impromptu Rock music history lessons and Jim Riordan's strong opinions on the 1960s were forcing to the surface whatever was buried deep inside me for decades. My search for Buddy Holly was clarifying things I had buried or purposefully blurred. I didn't know until Buddy came into my life that all these emotions and thoughts had been lurking below.

In 1970, more than a decade after the fateful crash in an Iowa farm field, the Kankakee Blackhawks Drum & Bugle Corps lined up in the staging area in preparation for a grand entry onto State Street to take part in the Veterans of Foreign Wars (VFW) State Convention Parade in Chicago. In 1970, the organization was enjoying its peak participation and membership because of the World War II generation, the men and women I believe saved the free world as we know it today.

Back then I was a young teenager getting ready to march in the VFW parade. I remember looking pretty sharp in my all-black military-style uniform, complete with a green and white sash across my shoulder and a black shako military hat with a tall white plume adorning my head. I carried a green marching snare drum with a silver stripe down the middle.

I loved Drum and Bugle Corps and had deep respect for the men and women who belonged to the VFW and a similar organization called the American Legion. As I said earlier, these people had saved the free world as we know it . . . right?

Before we headed into the parade, a decked-out VFW official accompanied by a Chicago Police officer approached our drum major, 17-year-old Teri Steinbach, and our adult corps director Earl Moran. The policeman looked especially grim, and a few minutes later I learned why. Drum Major Teri was a good friend. I could tell by her facial expressions and body movements that something was wrong. At the time I could only hear part of the conversation, but the way she looked at me when the police officer was speaking to her struck a nerve. As Drum Major, Teri was the highest ranking officer among the members of the Corps. I broke ranks and approached the assembled group to find out what was going on. Under any other circumstances Teri would have demanded I get back in line. But not on this day.

Teri's jaw tightened and her dark brown eyes narrowed as she quietly shared with me what she had just been told. The Students for a Democratic Society (SDS) and a splinter group called The Weather Underground were threatening to attack the flag bearers and tear down the American flags carried by the corps. Our flag was in the hands of sixteen-year-old Paula Burke, whose job it was to proudly carry Old Glory in front of the marching corps on a seven-foot steel pike with a shiny bronze eagle on top. Paula, whose red hair was pulled up and pinned under her shako, was accompanied by a young girl perhaps ten years old carrying a ceremonial saber. I remember being impressed by Teri's composure and presence of mind. I think this was the first time in our young lives that we were faced with a real-world situation that could result in bodily harm—or worse.

Teri and I watched Earl as the police officer approached Paula and told her of the threat. Paula began to cry. Teri, along with Dan Cote, Nick Eldred, Greg Kunde, Lonnie Netzel, my older brother Dave, and I—the oldest members of the corps—rushed to her side. We assured her that we would not let anyone touch her or our flag. Paula knew the assurances of a few teenage boys armed with drums and bugles would be of little help.

Gary Moore and his double-tenor drums (right) marches with the Cavaliers in Garfield, New Jersey, in July of 1972. As Jim Riordan told Gary, "This picture of you marching explains so much about you." *Wroblewski Family*

Performing with the Cavaliers (below) in Lincoln Park, Chicago, Illinois, in May of 1972. *Author*

At no point in my life did I feel more distant from the older members of my generation and all I thought they represented. At that moment, I hated them, their threat, their long hair . . . and their music.

Everyone walked back to their respective places and a few minutes later marched onto Wacker Drive before turning south onto State Street. As we did so, thousands of veterans lining both sides of the street erupted with applause. Normally I would have been excited beyond words. This time I barely noticed. My eyes were focused on Paula marching ahead of me. The flagpole was shaking in her hands and her shoulders were heaving up and down. I remember wondering if anyone in the audience realized that she was crying.

I scanned the crowd for any danger, but all I saw was a solid wave of veterans with their families, most standing at attention saluting the flag Paula carried as we passed, while some of the very old vets remained seated but were saluting nonetheless. In my young mind I compared what I saw in these men—appreciation, respect, and love of country—against the students who looked forward to disrupting our event and maybe even harming us. To the relief of everyone in the know, the parade went off without a problem.

After we finished marching we loaded into our busses and headed for home. I was stowing my gear in the overhead compartment when someone turned on WLS AM radio and "Sergeant Pepper" erupted throughout the bus. I felt the blood rush to my face as I turned and screamed, "Shut that crap off!" The music stopped immediately. Everyone looked at me as if seeing me for the first time. Yelling like that was way out of character for me. The bus ride home was eerily silent.

Over the years I have lost contact with most of the members of that small Drum & Bugle Corps because I left it to join The Cavaliers, headquartered at Logan Square in Chicago. I had not thought about those events of the summer of 1970 for decades. But I bet Paula remembers.

*   *   *

Tim Duggan had been trying his best to bring me up to Rock & Roll speed. He gave me several CDs he felt were important that I listen to and understand and he downloaded more than 100 songs onto my laptop when I was out of the office. The Beatles, Led Zeppelin, The Who, Bruce Springsteen, and a host of other Rock groups now graced my iTunes library.

For some strange and unexpected reason, talking with Tim and Jim and listening to the music of the 1960s brings back memories of Paula crying and the unfulfilled vision of a group of young political radicals who plotted to attack a helpless teenager because she carried an American flag.

Some of this 1960s-era music triggered long-forgotten memories and feelings of sadness, anger, and fear. Is this why I largely ignored the music of that time? The music was indeed a display of amazing talent, extreme creativity, and in a few cases outright genius. But in the recesses of my mind it also represented protest, anger, rebellion and violence against what I was raised to believe was good, wholesome, and important. At sixteen I thought we were fighting in Vietnam so that others could be free. Was I wrong? Were they? Or was it like most issues in life: we find truth only when we are open to hear it, and it usually resides not on either end of the spectrum but somewhere in the middle.

Now I got it. The realization is taking firmer form. I put Rock & Roll out of my head for most of my life because I have been (unfairly and inaccurately) tying this together with the protests and violence of the sixties and early seventies.

I recall with great sadness the way our soldiers were treated at home only because they answered the call of their nation and wore the uniform of the United States military. I remember clearly (and with complete disdain), the raves of the SDS and the violence of the Weather Underground. To this day I still do not understand why their leaders were not convicted and locked away or why they are still, in some circles, hailed as heroes. Bill Ayers and Bernardine Dohrn have been in the national news lately because of the campaign and election of Barack Obama. Every time I see them on the air I wonder, "How did they escape a jail sentence after plotting to set off bombs?"

Jim/Levi Riordan romanticizes the sixties as a time of enlightenment and an important turning point in our culture. He is convinced the era produced great accomplishments, but also represents opportunities lost. I see it as a very sad time filled with anger, misunderstanding, and the clash of what Tom Brokaw labeled "The Greatest Generation" against their children of the "Baby Boom Generation" who, for reasons their parents did not fully understand, were rebelling against them. Even today, neither group seems to have much comprehension of what drives the other. I gravitate to the opposite end of the spectrum from where Jim sits, sympathizing with our aging veterans' lack of understanding of why their kids turned such rage against them.

All of this, of course, was merely back story to the questions I was seeking to answer: "What would Buddy have thought about the direction of the culture that his musical lineage partly represents?"

"What would Buddy have been like had the chartered plane arrived at its destination and Buddy raved on through the sixties and beyond?"

"Would Buddy's influence have changed the direction of that momentous decade, or would the culture have pulled Buddy along in a more radical direction?"

"Was the momentum toward conflict so strong that no one person or his music could have stopped it?"

Much of this was coming into focus forty years after the parade in Chicago and the threats from the Weather Underground while I sat listening to The Who sing "My Generation." This music is amazing! And I missed it all even though it was on radio stations and splashed across magazines and television. I grew up in the middle of it and barely noticed. I missed a decade or more of music because I attached the actions of a few to the music permeating the masses—and then shut it out.

Shame on me for allowing the actions of a few angry domestic terrorists to chase me away from the music of my youth. More importantly . . . shame on them . . . for all of it.

Chapter 27

Baby won't you come out tonight

"**Gary**, you really need to go to Lubbock," my wife Arlene said to me one morning during our drive to the office. "You should try to meet some of Buddy's family members face-to-face and visit the Buddy Holly Center."

"I know, I know," I responded a little more sharply than usual. "And I'm running out of time. I'm less than thirty days away from my deadline."

"You have been talking about it for months. You better pack a bag," Arlene said. "How can you finish this book and not visit his hometown in Texas?"

"I can't, and I know that," I sighed. There was so much to do and so little time. Resistance was futile. I was going to Lubbock.

We arrived at the office and within five minutes I was sitting at my desk calling Southwest Airlines' reservation line. I always fly Southwest. It is hands down my favorite airline.

"Southwest Airlines, this is Peggy Sue. How may I assist you today," said the chipper voice on the other end of the phone. (And as Dave Barry might say, I am not making this up.)

"Did you say Peggy Sue?" I asked.

"Yes, Peggy Sue," she responded. "How may I help you today?"

I started laughing. Fortunately, the stranger named Peggy Sue laughed right along with me. And she knew why both of us were chuckling on the phone. "My parents were huge Buddy Holly fans," she offered without me having to offer a word of explanation. "They couldn't wait to have a little girl and name her Peggy Sue. That's me!"

"You have to be kidding me. I'm flying to Lubbock, Texas, to finish up interviews and last minute research on a Buddy Holly book."

"Really?" asked Peggy Sue. "Well, you called the right place. We can deliver you to Lubbock no problem, and provide all the peanuts you can eat," she replied. I could almost see the smile in her voice.

We took care of business and booked my flight. When we finished a few minutes later Peggy Sue continued our conversation where we had left off. "I can remember my dad rocking me to sleep singing Peggy Sue," she said with a special fondness in her voice. "As a gift, friends of our family took an old forty-five of 'Peggy Sue,' painted the black vinyl gold, and mounted it on a plaque with the words, 'Welcome to the world, Peggy Sue,' inscribed on it. My family—let's just say we were big Buddy fans and we still are to this day."

"Peggy Sue, I am delighted you answered the phone tonight," I replied with real enthusiasm. "Do you mind if I recount this story in my book?"

"Are you serious?" she asked before matching my own enthusiasm. "Not at all! Just be sure to tell everyone Peggy Sue says hi!"

I thanked her and hung up. Buddy's impact, large and small, is everywhere. No matter where I go, everywhere I turn I find Buddy.

I'm going to Lubbock.

Wish I could meet him.

Chapter 28

We're all looking for someone to love down here

You already know that I love Texas and Texans, so you know I have been looking forward to my trip to Lubbock for quite a while. I rose early in the morning and pulled out my clothes for the trip. My flight was from Chicago Midway Airport to Lubbock, by way of Dallas. I dreaded the moment I would kiss Arlene and say goodbye. (As I get older it gets harder and harder to say goodbye, even for a short time.) I've been all over Texas but never to Lubbock. My mother lived in Amarillo, a little north of Lubbock, for a short time in the late 1930s, but that was my only connection.

I checked Lubbock weather as I packed my bag. It was hot. Not heat wave hot, but too hot for a sports coat. "Jeans? Check! Boots? Check! Hawaiian shirt? Check!" I said aloud, as I always did before leaving for a trip.

"Sports coat? Check! Dockers? Check!" laughed Arlene, who had snuck up behind me. She was holding my tweed sports coat and khakis on hangers, one in each hand.

"What?" I asked defensively.

"Just because I'm not with you doesn't mean you can dress like that!" she exclaimed. "The Hawaiian shirt and cowboy boots may not be the right look for you in Texas," she continued, extending her arms to hand me the hangars. "You want to be taken seriously, right? You're the one who trains salespeople and speaks to them about the importance of appearance when you're not writing books. Dress for success, right?"

I was going to protest, but realized that just because I packed them didn't mean I had to wear them. "Yes, of course, Arlene." I responded. "Should I also pack my tux?"

"Boots or no boots?" she asked with a smile.

"You know I always wear boots with my tux," I grinned back with a sly wink. I have been married long enough to understand exactly what she meant.

"You are such a Texas wannabee," she replied, shaking her head.

I shrugged and turned back to my garment bag. "I just like boots. You know that."

We said our goodbyes and I headed for Midway hoping I'd have time in Dallas to eat some Texas barbeque at the airport. The flight from Midway was uneventful and we landed to moderate Texas summer weather: 85 degrees. I collected my bag, stopped at the rental car counter, and made the short walk to my car. The sky was a radiant blue, the sun was bright, and I was in the Lone Star State. I love Texas. Does it get any better than this?

I decided on the flight that the first place I would visit was the City of Lubbock Cemetery. Three things jumped out at me during the drive to Buddy's final resting place: the flatness of the terrain, the lack of trees, and the color green that goes along with them. I'm a northern Illinois boy, so I'm used to flat, but the lack of green always strikes me. I drove through the entrance off East 31st Street and pulled over to the side. The cemetery was much larger than I anticipated. How long it will take me to find Buddy? I wondered. Would I even find Buddy?

I put the car back in drive and eased my way forward and within a few seconds spotted a sign on my right that read "Buddy Holly Grave Site." An arrow pointed to my left. "That was easy," I thought. I parked, took six steps to cross the narrow street, and nearly stumbled over him. I was standing at the foot of the resting place for the man who has been living in my head for most of a year.

The sign not far inside the City of Lubbock Cemetery. *Author*

"Hey, Buddy," I mumbled, looking around to make sure no one watching. I consciously decided to speak to him out loud. "My name is Gary. I'm the guy who's been stalking you for months." I laughed, but it felt odd doing so in a cemetery. "John Mueller introduced me to you in Cedar Falls, Iowa, last February. Do you remember?" I looked around again, slightly embarrassed. Had I lost my mind? I was standing in a strange city talking to a headstone as if I was asking a waiter for an iced tea. To make matters worse, I was waiting for him to answer.

"I am sure you know John, right?" It was starting to feel comfortable talking to Buddy this way. "Buddy, do you realize the positive and profound impact you continue to have on people? Do you understand how much people still love and appreciate you?"

I looked around again to make sure I was alone. It felt good to talk to Buddy. Until now, my conversations had mostly been in my head, and then on paper. Now they were face-to-face, so to speak.

I pulled out my iPhone and snapped a picture of his stone. I was posting it on my Facebook page and wondered at the same time whether it was wrong. I shook my head and said aloud, "This is alright. I'm allowing others to visit Buddy's resting place with me." I checked the page to make sure the image was posted. It was.

"Your music is amazing, but you know that," I said to Buddy. "Your songs still live, and through your music, you live on in our hearts and minds with us. But I'm coming to believe it's not your music but your heart, which beats through your songs and touches the very depths of our souls, that draws us close to you. You bring a lot of joy to others, Buddy. And after all these years, your popularity is growing."

I glanced down at my iPhone to discover that people were already responding to the picture I had posted from the cemetery on my Facebook page. It had only been up there for a minute or so. One was a posting to me from Taryn Serwatowski. "True love of my life! Too bad I was born too late!" she wrote, attaching a picture of her shoulder with the large tattoo of Buddy's smiling face, complete with his black glasses. I had interviewed Taryn several weeks ago. She is a graduate student in her mid-twenties. Buddy was in this cemetery for than more than twenty

Buddy's gravestone. *Author*

years before she was born, and yet he had impacted her so deeply she had permanently memorialized his face on her shoulder and back. Tattoos, like diamonds, are forever.

"Buddy, can you believe this?" I laughed out loud. "I know your picture is everywhere, but how about on Taryn's shoulder?" I pointed my iPhone at his headstone as if Buddy were able to see it.

I continued to make small talk with Buddy. It felt as though he was listening. When I had said all I needed to say, I offered my goodbyes. It was time to find my hotel and check in. I turned toward my car but felt pulled back. I typed my hotel name into my iPhone map. Five miles.

I turned again to leave. Again, I felt pulled back.

"I'm here," I wrote in a brief email to John Mueller, attached the headstone photo, and sent it. A moment later I did the same to my publisher, Ted Savas, and Arlene. My iPhone rang thirty seconds later.

"Hi Arlene," I answered. Suddenly I felt very emotional. She brings that side out in me. My wife is the only person I feel comfortable allowing to see my emotions, regardless of what they are.

"How does Buddy like your boots?"

"I think Buddy is a loafer guy."

"Are you okay?"

"Yes. Why wouldn't I be?"

"It's me, Gary," Arlene said softly. "I don't completely understand, but I see what is going on . . . what you're going through."

"I want to play him a song, Arlene. I want to play 'Hey, Buddy' for him," I continued, knowing full well that at that moment I sounded like a child.

"Then do it," she said. "I wonder if John has ever brought his guitar out to the cemetery and played it for him?" Before I could reply she answered her own question. "Probably not. That would be a Gary thing to do." She paused. "Play it for him."

"If John hasn't, I want to be here when he does." I paused and looked around. "I'll call you back."

"You're going to do it, aren't you?" she asked, already knowing the answer.

"Yes. I'll call you back."

I pulled the earphones out of my iPhone and turned up the volume, clicked on the speaker then clicked on 'Hey, Buddy.' I was surprised how loud it was. The guitar opening began and I said, "Hey, Buddy, this is for you from John Mueller and all the rest of us who love you."

The song I love and that had sent me on this wild ride poured out of my iPhone over Buddy's tombstone, covering his resting place like a beautiful blanket. I felt the need to dance, but I saw groundskeepers coming my way. They'll call the psych ward, I thought. I decided not to dance, but it was hard.

Once the song ended I knew it was time to leave. And as odd as it sounds, I felt "released" and now able to walk away.

"Hey, Buddy," I said before heading for my car. "I'll stop by again Saturday morning."

*   *   *

I woke up the next day, a Friday morning, to the sound of cars driving past the hotel. "How many times did Buddy drive by here?" I wondered. I got out of bed, showered, dressed, and headed to the Buddy Holly Center (BHC).

I smiled when I spotted a giant pair of glasses sitting on the ground facing the parking lot. The sign proudly announced BUDDY HOLLY CENTER.

"Must be the place," I said aloud.

The Buddy Holly Center is located in a beautiful old building that was once a train depot. The center is largely supported by funding from the city of Lubbock, and for that the world owes the people of Lubbock a real debt of gratitude. Their generosity has given fans from all over the world a place where we can come to learn more about the life of Buddy Holly.

I walked into the lobby, which hosts a large red neon sign of Buddy's signature. "My name is Gary," I announced to Trish, the girl sitting at the front desk. "I'm here to meet with Jacquie." I handed Trish my card. Before she could call, Jacqueline Bober walked out with her hand extended and a big smile on her face.

In front of the Buddy Holly Center in Lubbock, Texas . . .

"You must be Gary! We've been expecting you," Jacquie said as she reached out to shake my hand. "What would you like to see or do first?"

"I'm not sure," I replied. "Maybe we can just sit for a few moments and talk." Jacquie led me to her conference room, where we made the sort of small talk strangers usually do when they first meet. "How long have you been with the Buddy Holly Center, Jacquie?"

"It will be two years in October."

"You're the curator of the center?" I asked.

"Yes, I am."

I had to ask the question. "Were you a fan?"

"I was aware of Buddy," Jacquie answered while nodding. "My parents were fans and through them I became familiar with much of his music. After being here for almost two years, I have certainly become a Buddy Holly fan!" she said smiling.

Jacqueline Bober is a trained museum professional. She graduated from Westminster College in New Wilmington, PA (Bachelors of Science in Biology) and then obtained her Master of Arts in Museum

Science at Texas Tech University, where she met her husband. She worked outside her profession for a few years as a business manager in the medical field, but when the opportunity to apply for the position as curator at the Buddy Holly Center became available, she took it. It didn't take me long to appreciate that the center is more than fortunate to have a person of Jacquie's qualifications at the helm. And there was something else. Every once in a while I meet someone I feel I have known for a long time and feel an instant connection. I felt that with Jacquie right away.

"Did you ever make contact with Bill Griggs?" Jacquie asked.

"I did, thanks." I answered. "Bill's wife Sharon said that if Bill is feeling up to it, she would try to bring him down today."

"I hope he's feeling well enough to come, Gary. Bill is our 'go to' guy here for anything Buddy," confirmed Jacquie. "He made fifties rock & roll his life's work and his main focus is Buddy Holly. He's known as the world's leading Buddy Holly expert, and there is no one better. I have no idea what we would do without Bill."

. . . and with Buddy's oversized glasses. *Author*

"Jacquie—Bill's not well, is he?" I asked.

"No, he's not at all well, but sometimes you would never know it." Jacquie's smile vanished and she turned to look out the window. "Bill was diagnosed with cancer. It began as colon cancer, but I think it has spread."

"Oh, I am so sorry!" I replied. "What's the prognosis?"

At that moment several voices and laughter erupted from the foyer. Jacquie's smile returned. "Let's go meet Bill!"

Bill Griggs is known far and wide for his extensive collection of Buddy Holly items and for his vast knowledge on the subject. He is the author of *Buddy Holly: A Collector's Guide* and runs his website www.rockin50s.com. Bill is also the founder of the Buddy Holly Memorial Society, which boasts in impressive membership in thirty-four countries. Bill knows Buddy.

We all stood out in the foyer and listened as Bill offered up a stunning array of facts, figures, dates, and details to any question about Buddy I asked him.

"Bill?" Jacquie interrupted. "Would you mind giving Gary a tour of the exhibit?"

"Of course," Bill agreed, leading us into a beautiful exhibit room shaped like the body of an acoustic guitar. Buddy's music played softly in the background. What an amazing tribute to Lubbock's favorite son.

The first presentation case contained items from Buddy's early childhood. I was immediately drawn to a Cub Scout uniform. I looked up and caught Bill's eye. "I wore that same uniform when I was a Cub Scout."

Bill smiled and I went back to browsing the display case. The uniform brought back memories for me. My mom took of photo of me in my Cub Scout uniform sitting at my first orange sparkle drum set. For the first time this man I have been so actively pursuing, the late great Buddy Holly, seemed . . . not unlike . . . me. A Cub Scout and a young grade school musician. The connection I had been feeling with Buddy deepened. I thought about Ron McIntosh and Jeff Frederickson, two guitar players from my grade school garage band. I wondered where they were now. I hadn't thought of them in years.

Jacqueline Bober (right), Curator of the Buddy Holly Center, with education coordinator Lisa Howe (left), and Sarah Collins, assistant to Ms. Bober. *Buddy Holly Center*

"Gary, this next cabinet has items from his later childhood. Drawings, his report cards, and so on," Bill announced, pointing to second display case.

The report cards looked like my report cards that we found after my mother died. I have them at home somewhere. Buddy was a normal kid. He was a Texas grade school teacher's student. He was a son, a brother. He was like the rest of us. What else would I have thought? Buddy was an ordinary kid who went on to do extraordinary things.

The exhibits were very personal and deeply touching. I shifted my gaze to his drawings of horses, clay figures, a few leather items he crafted. Buddy was like all the other children of the 50s and 60s. A lot like me. Maybe like you. He was older than me—18 years older—but it was obvious he was raised much as I had been.

The other exhibits didn't grab me the same way. For some reason I was stuck back at his grade school and junior high life—until we came to the glasses.

When I saw them I looked up at Bill. He knew exactly what I was thinking. "These are the glasses Buddy was wearing during the crash," he said with a nod of his head. "The lenses were busted and missing and the frame was cracked."

"We've repaired the cracked frame, but have done nothing else," Jacquie added.

All three of us stood staring at the iconic black glasses that Buddy made world-famous. The glasses on display are not a replica or similar to the glasses Buddy wore. They are the glasses Buddy wore.

"Someone put them in an envelope and tucked them away in an evidence locker in Cerro Gordo County, Iowa," explained Bill. "They sat there until a sheriff found them in 1980 while looking for something else unrelated to the 1959 crash. He called to tell me. During the conversation the sheriff stopped and said 'wait . . . it's running.' I asked him 'What's running?' and he answered, 'Richardson's watch.'" Bill paused a moment. "Can you believe that? After all those years, when the sheriff picked up the Big Bopper's self-winding watch, it began running."

We finished the tour at the acoustic guitar Buddy was tuning in the famous Dick Cole photograph that graces the dust jacket of this book. I looked at the guitar and then at Dick's photo hanging on the wall.

"Yes," Bill said. "That's the guitar in the picture. What else would you like to know?"

I didn't reply. Honestly, I was mesmerized, staring at the guitar and listening to the notes as Buddy picked the strings and adjusted the tuning keys.

"Gary?" Bill asked. "What else would you like to know?"

"Sorry, Bill." The look on his face told me he fully understood. I bet he had seen this repeated countless times over the years. "Well," I began, "Let's start at the end. Let's talk about the accident, rumors, conspiracy theories—that sort of thing. What do you know about their origins?"

I think my question threw him. It was not really what he was expecting right out of the gate. "What exactly are you looking for?" Bill asked.

I began with the story of how the lineman gassing my plane in Mason City in 1991 insisted the wrecked plane was stored in a nearby hangar, and ended with my conversation with Barb Dwyer and her curious comment, "The truth has never been told about what really happened." I also explained that I was a pilot and a former charter and flight school operator.

"How did this silly rumor that Buddy shot the pilot begin?" I asked.

"In the spring of 1959, Albert Juhl was plowing his rented field at the crash site and unearthed a handgun," began Bill. "He brought it to the sheriff and told the sheriff where he found it. The sheriff examined the gun and observed that it had been fired. 'There is a spent cartridge,' the sheriff told him. 'It still works,' Juhl told the sheriff. 'I fired it into the air!' So the sheriff discovered that the gun belonged to Buddy and the rumors began from there. The farmer fired the only shot from that gun. Not Buddy," Bill affirmed.

"What do you think caused the crash?" I asked.

"Icing," he said quickly and with authority. "Icing brought down that plane. Old man Dwyer has it and buried it."

Both statements surprised me. "Well," I began slowly. The last thing I wanted to do was disagree with the world's leading authority on Buddy Holly. "I disagree on both counts," I finally replied. Bill shot me a look of surprise that made me feel as though no one ever disagrees with Bill Griggs about anything related to Buddy.

"You disagree with what?" Bill asked.

"I don't believe it was icing that brought down the plane, and I don't think Dwyer has the plane."

"I *know* he has it." Bill's tone was sharp.

"Have you seen it?" I asked.

"No, but I have spoken to people who have, and who have also seen a few of the instruments," he replied quickly. "Dwyer has the plane."

"How do you know they are from the Bonanza that crashed with Buddy?" I asked. "Maybe they're similar. There are lots of old airplane instruments around." The look on Bill's face told me he wanted to hear more, so I continued. "I don't know for certain, of course, but I don't believe Dwyer has the plane. Barb Dwyer insinuated to me that the truth was in that plane and she spoke like a woman fiercely defending her husband's honor. If they have the plane and Barb is right, why didn't they produce it decades ago to defend Jerry Dwyer's decision to let Roger Peterson take off that night?"

"Jerry told me he was going to write a book on the fiftieth anniversary," answered Bill.

"Then he's late, right?" I replied with a chuckle. Bill didn't join me in the laugh. "Good thing he doesn't have my publisher! I'm worried about being a week to ten days late with my manuscript. Jerry is almost two years late. Barb told me Jerry is writing a book. I told her I'd help and that I would even assist them in finding a publisher. She just kept repeating that the truth had never been told—over and over. What truth do you think she's speaking of, Bill?" I asked.

I waited for an answer but only got a shrug in reply. I continued, "The truth is that no one knows the truth, right? All the witnesses perished in the crash. The CAB published a detailed report, and I have heard and read nothing that would make me believe they were wrong in their conclusions. Most of the people who claim the CAB was wrong are not pilots and have no aviation background or experience. I have both."

"The CAB is wrong. It was a sloppy report," Bill insisted.

Bill's observation was interesting. "A sloppy report doesn't mean that the report and findings were wrong, though," I countered. "Anyway, we're not going to solve it here. None of the eyewitnesses are present or available for questioning. If Barb Dwyer is right, they should produce the plane and silence the critics—don't you think?"

Bill remained silent. I looked over to my right and I saw what looked like a bedroom. "What's that?" I asked Jacquie, hoping I had not upset Bill and desperate to change the subject.

"Come. Let me show you," she answered quickly. She felt the tension as well. Jacquie and I walked over to the bedroom exhibit. Bill did not join us.

"This is Buddy's?" I asked.

"Yes, it is," Jacquie answered. Her voice softened. "This is his furniture and the clothes laid out on his bed also belonged to him." The reverence in her voice was palpable.

We both stood there staring at the room. Neither of us said a word for several minutes.

John Mueller (left) with Buddy's brother Travis Holley. *Author*

"Travis, Buddy's brother, was in here after we set up this display. He stood there," she said, pointing to a spot near the bed. "He was looking around and made the comment that it was much neater than when Buddy was here." Jacquie smiled. "I could tell Travis was becoming emotional. I think the Holleys were, and continue to be, a tight-knit family. We love them all."

"We think of Buddy as this larger-than-life celebrity who died more than fifty years ago," I said, "but to Travis and the rest of the Holley family he was a brother, a son, and an uncle. How do you get over that kind of loss?" Jacquie understood it was a rhetorical question and didn't respond. "This display is very touching," I added.

"I change the clothes laid out on the bed with the seasons. These, of course, are Buddy's summer clothes. We'll be getting out his fall clothes soon," Jacquie explained. "I'll come in early one morning and put these clothes away and lay out clothes appropriate for the season."

I imagined Jacquie picking out Buddy's clothes and laying them out on the bed with the care and attention only a mom can provide. Jacquie has a teenage son. How can she change the clothes without thinking about her own child? Without thinking about how life is so fragile, and that all of us are only one accident away from losing our loved ones.

"I can see how this could make Travis and his family emotional," I confessed. "He must really miss Buddy. We know Buddy as this musical prodigy and Rock and Roll pioneer bigger than life, but to Travis—he just misses his younger brother Buddy." Jacquie and I walked away from Buddy's bedroom in a completely different mood. When we returned, Bill and I talked more about Buddy, and then he and Sharon said their goodbyes and left. They are wonderful people and it was delightful to spend this time with them at the Buddy Holly Center.

I walked through the main exhibit room one more time before heading back to my hotel. I was so happy I got to meet Jacquie, Bill, and Sharon, and see the center. But I was also disappointed. I had planned on meeting several of the Holley family members. Unfortunately, only one—Buddy's nephew Eddie Weir—came to the center. Eddie was great to talk with and a very nice guy, but no one else showed up. Jacquie had sensed my disappointment as I was leaving. "I think they are just tired of all the attention, Gary," she said with a sad smile on her face. "They are great people and a wonderful family, but they have been dealing with all the questions for more than fifty years."

The Buddy Holly Center is a beautiful tribute to Buddy. It is tastefully arranged and a treasure for Buddy fans. Thank you Jacqueline Bober and the people of Lubbock, Texas. I am truly grateful and profoundly touched.

*   *   *

I rose early Saturday morning, packed my few things, and headed to the cemetery to say goodbye before catching my flight home.

Chapter 29

To help us make it through

Arlene and I attended the wedding of Sarah Shirk and Paul Fuller. Sarah is the daughter of our dear friends Rob and Tracey Shirk. Arlene and Tracey grew up together in Waterloo and Rob and I became instant friends the moment we met in 1973. We have enjoyed a long and enduring relationship even though we live 350 miles apart. The Shirks are more like family than friends.

"Since we are going to be in Waterloo for the wedding," Arlene mentioned a few weeks before, "this would be a good time to get your trip to Clear Lake and the Surf Ballroom out of the way."

It sounded so irreverent when she said it that way, but I knew what she meant. She was trying to be efficient and she was right: it would be a good time to go. "Great!" I responded. "We can drive over in the morning and drive home from there. But I'm not going to get it out of the way, Arlene," I replied, perhaps a bit defensively. "This is an important trip. And of course, I want you to come with me."

"We?" Arlene sounded surprised. "Speaking French? I'm not going. We're going to have two cars there. I'm driving out on Wednesday to help Tracey prepare for the wedding and you aren't coming until Friday morning. I'm spending the day with my mom on Sunday while you go to Clear Lake. We'll meet somewhere on the way home."

"Then I'll get Rob to go along with me," I answered. "This is too important. This is something you share with others."

"Sure, get Rob to go with you if you want to cause World War III," said Arlene. "He's going to have family in town and Tracey isn't going to understand why you need someone to hold your hand as you walk into a cornfield. You're gonna have to go this one alone, big boy."

She had me on that one. But, I thought, there will be 250 people at the wedding. Someone will want to tag along to see the Surf and the site of the plane crash, right?

I'm an extrovert. An extreme extrovert. My Myers-Briggs Personality Profiler result (a test that classifies personality type—you can find it on the Internet and take it yourself) is ENFP. That means Extrovert, Intuitive, Feeler, Preceptor. I am heavy on the "E". I hate being alone and hate doing anything by myself. If I cannot find someone to have lunch with, often I don't eat. If I were alone on a desert island, I would probably starve to death—but not before going stark raving mad from loneliness and boredom. In the strictest sense, the differences between an extrovert and introvert are determined by what gives them energy. In my case, I gain energy from being with others and I drain energy when I am alone. I don't like being or doing anything alone. It truly wears me out. I know that must sound strange coming from an author, but I rarely write alone. It is something I do alone in my head, but I usually write in a room while others are present. The more, the merrier.

The wedding was perfect and the bride was simply stunning. When I mentioned to several people during the course of the evening that I was driving north to Clear Lake to visit the Buddy Holly crash site and hopefully the Surf Ballroom, they all looked at me like I was brain damaged.

*   *   *

On Sunday morning I loaded my luggage into the car, said my goodbyes, and set out for Clear Lake alone. "So I drain off a little energy," I told myself. "I can do this alone."

First, however, I stopped in Waterloo to see the old Electric Park Ballroom where Dick Cole snapped his famous photo of Buddy sitting on the freezer tuning his guitar. It was on the way to Clear Lake and I thought I should take a look.

I made the thirty-minute drive from Independence (where Arlene's mom lives) to Waterloo, easily found the old ballroom, and pulled into the parking lot. The ballroom's portico extends out from the front door with a neon light (turned off) proclaiming "Electric Park" in a half-circle on the top. I snapped a few pictures and walked toward the door, hoping I could catch a glimpse of the stage inside. Still, it was a Sunday and I was fairly certain the place was locked and empty. You can imagine my surprise when I approached the door and it opened! I caught the door and stepped inside. It took a few moments for my eyes to adjust to the darker interior.

Standing in front of me was a bearded man with the darkest eyes I had ever seen. He was just standing there, leaning on a mop.

"Thank you," I said. "I didn't expect anyone to be here."

The front of the Electric Park Ballroom in Waterloo, Iowa. *Author*

From left to right: Maria Elena Holly, Buddy Holly, Jackie Everly, and Phil Everly (of the Everly Brothers) in the El Chico restaurant in New York City. The exact date is uncertain, but it was on or after August 30, 1958. *Steve Bonner*

Without asking why I was here, the bearded man did a half-turn and tilted his head. "This is the original stage," he began. "Buddy played here July of 1958 and made a lot of friends in town. They took him water skiing the next day."

I didn't know what to say, so for several seconds I didn't say a single word. In fact, the skin crawled on my arms. "How did you know why I was here?" I asked.

"You have that look about you," answered the bearded man. "They show up here all the time and always ask the same questions. They all want to know if that is the stage Buddy played on. Most ask if they can go up and stand there." He motioned toward the stage. "Go on."

So, I did. I walked up and stood on the old stage and looked around. It was a beautiful old place. "Has it changed much since 1958?" I asked.

"I don't rightly know," he responded. "I'm sure there have been some changes." He shrugged and looked around. "Not many, though. Before you ask, there's the kitchen," he said, pointing to a door off to the side of the large dance floor. "I don't know where Ol' Dick Cole snapped that photo that made him so famous. You'll have to look around and figure it out for yourself." The bearded man sounded like I was beginning to wear my welcome thin. I think he was anxious to finish mopping and get home.

"You're kidding, right?" I asked.

"Kidding about what?"

"How did you know I'd want to see the kitchen?" I wondered whether Arlene called ahead.

This time he sighed before answering. "I told you already. You have that look. I've seen it lots of times through the years. You all ask the same questions."

I walked back into the kitchen but had no idea where the photo was taken. It looked like what it was then and is today: a kitchen. I was hoping to see something or feel something—maybe know right away, "Ah, that's where Dick snapped the photo!" In that regard I admit disappointment. I

A view of the stage where Buddy played in 1958—the same concert photographer Dick Cole attended as a fan and where he captured the iconic image of Buddy on the freezer tuning his guitar. *Author*

remained a couple of minutes, walked around inside a bit, and walked back out.

I was taking a final look around inside the ballroom when I noticed a unique painting of Buddy hanging on the wall. The bearded man saw me staring at it.

"Local artist painted it," he said while leaning on his mop. "That's all I know about it."

I looked back at this bearded stranger, caught his eye, and thought really hard, *How long will it take me to get to Clear Lake?* I waited for several seconds but he didn't answer. Actually I was relieved. I was beginning to think he could read my mind.

"Thanks for letting me in," I told him as I headed for the door.

"Are you driving to Clear Lake?" he asked.

I stopped, turned around, and began laughing. "I have that look, right?"

"Right," he said. For the first time he offered me a big smile.

I smiled back. "I guess I am."

"Never been there," he replied. Before I could ask him why not, he had turned around and was busy mopping—and laughing quietly.

Even with the door closed behind me and half way across the parking lot I could hear his laugh echoing inside my head. He was laughing at me. There was something Stephen King-like about the entire experience inside that old ballroom. Suddenly I had the overpowering urge to have Arlene with me.

I climbed back into my car, reached back and pulled my seatbelt tight, and turned the key. It was nice seeing the stage and the kitchen, but what struck me the most was the size of the ballroom. It seemed so small. I guessed the capacity was about 800 (and later learned it was closer to 1,200), but that would be jammed to the gills. Buddy was well on his way to being a national celebrity in the summer of 1958, and this is the type of venue he was playing? We tend to think of larger venues and even stadiums when thinking of Rock legends, so it serves as a good reminder about how new Rock & Roll was when Buddy was out on the circuit in the late 1950s A capacity crowd like that at that time must have been considered pretty good. Buddy was one of the pioneers who made larger audiences possible for those who followed in his footsteps, but he didn't get to experience or enjoy them himself during his short reign at the top.

I was only a few miles from the Gallagher-Bluedorn Performing Arts Center at the University of Northern, Iowa, where John Mueller played for two sold-out nights. The seating capacity there was about 1,700. More than five decades later Mueller was selling out back-to-back shows to larger crowds than many of the places Buddy played. The Mueller event in Columbus, Ohio, was several times larger again. Did Buddy ever play in front of that many people? I didn't know.

Chapter 30

These blue days

The drive to Clear Lake was roughly ninety miles from Electric Park. I pulled out of the parking lot and called Arlene. As usual, her phone rang but she didn't answer. Arlene has this idea that her phone is for her convenience, not mine. Go figure. So who could I call? I called my daughter Tara Beth and got her voicemail. I called both my sons, Toby in California and Travis in Chicago. Neither answered. Both, I'm sure, were still sleeping. How could I make a drive that long without talking to someone? I pulled out a CD and listened to Buddy and John Mueller. I thought about calling John but decided not to because he had performed the night before in Modesto, California.

I'm not sure what I expected from my visit to the Electric Park Ballroom. As an author I wanted to feel something special, and then write about what I felt. But I admit I left disappointed. Electric Park was interesting, but it didn't stir any real emotions. Perhaps I was expecting too much.

About a half an hour outside Waterloo driving north on Highway 218 I passed a sign for Shell Rock. That's where Stacey, the librarian from Batavia, is from. I wisely decided not to bother her. What would I have said? "Happy Sunday morning! Hope I didn't wake you. I'm passing through Shell Rock, and just wanted to let you know." Instead, I opened the Facebook app on my iPhone and posted on my Facebook page,

"Passing through Shell Rock, Iowa, headed for Clear Lake." Then I recalled signing the pledge spearheaded by Oprah to stop texting while driving, I felt guilty about breaking it and put the phone on the seat and shook my head. It really is a dumb and dangerous thing to do. No more of that!

I was running low on gas, so pulled off the highway at Charles City for some gas at the Kwik Trip. A middle-aged man in a white T-shirt with an Iowa Hawkeyes cap on was filling his tank next to me. I got my own pump going and turned to face him, leaning back against my car.

"Hi! How ya doing?" I asked with a wide smile. It's just my nature and as an extrovert, I needed company. I can't help it. He glanced over his shoulder to see if I was talking to someone else, and when it was apparent I was not, gave me a "Why are you talking to me?" glare. I held my smile and he finally nodded slightly in my direction. "Driving out to Clear Lake," I continued. The poor guy couldn't tighten his gas cap fast enough. Within five seconds he was speeding out of the station. "His loss," I grumbled under my breath.

The gas was still pumping, so I pulled out my phone and checked Facebook. Stacey the librarian had already responded: "Tell everyone in Shell Rock I said 'Hi!'"

I finished filling my tank and climbed back into the driver's seat. Before pulling out I tried calling Tim. No answer. I dialed Jim (aka Levi). Same result. I thought about calling my publisher, Ted Savas (I have his cell phone number), but was afraid that if I woke him this early he might change his mind and not publish my book. I was beginning to get very tired.

I pulled out of the Kwik Trip, but not before sticking my iPhone under the passenger seat. I figured it was the best way to keep my pledge to Oprah—and reach Clear Lake alive.

I had no idea what to expect, but found Clear Lake to be a gorgeous community! The lake was full of sailboats racing around under a brisk breeze and a sun that was finally beginning to show its face. I drove up North Shore Drive, forgetting for a moment why I was there . . . and there it was.

The Surf Ballroom.

The legendary ballroom in Clear Lake, Iowa. *Author*

I pulled into the parking lot and jumped out of the car. The bright blue letters on the side looked just like all the photos I had seen. I walked up to the door and was reaching for it when I spotted the sign: "Sunday—Closed."

Oh, man!

Okay, okay, I thought. Let's walk around and see what we can see. (I was so desperate for company by this point that I began speaking as if someone was with me.) I looked through the glass doors but couldn't see much. There was a bench out front, so I took a seat and sat for fifteen minutes or so. During that quarter-hour, five different cars slowed down as they passed and snapped pictures of the Surf sign. Hmm. "Why would they do that?" I wondered. The only thing I could come up with was because Buddy's last gig was here. What else could it be? After all this time this place is still important to people. I understand it now, but would not have understood it at all but for my evening at John Mueller's "Winter Dance Party."

My hypothesis about the intent of the anonymous photographers was confirmed a few minutes later when a minivan with plates from Ohio pulled into the lot. Two kids jumped out ahead of their parents and ran up to a small monument in the front of the building commemorating Buddy, Ritchie, the Big Bopper, and pilot Roger Peterson. Near the top in big letters it says, "In Memory of Rock N Roll Legends." Below it are these words:

> The above legends
> played their last concert
> at the Surf Ballroom,
> Clear Lake, Iowa,
> on February 2, 1959.
> Their earthly life
> tragically ended
> in a plane crash
> 5.2 miles northwest of
> the Mason City Airport,
> February 3, 1959.
> Their music lives on

"Cool!" exclaimed the oldest, a boy who looked to be about nine years old. The middle child, a girl maybe all of six, stood stock straight and said with real enthusiasm and authority, "This is their grave. They are in the ground here." She folded her hands as if she was beginning to pray. That was really touching. This young girl thought the granite memorial was a tombstone.

Mom and Dad arrived with another youngster in tow a few seconds later. "Mom, is this their grave?" asked the oldest.

"No, I don't think so," she answered. "This is just a monument with their names on it so we don't forget them."

"I'm hungry," whined the youngest, perhaps four or five years old. "Can we eat?"

"OK, OK," answered the dad.

The parents herded the kids back into the minivan and started the engine and Buddy's "Not Fade Away" cranked up from inside. I was

The memorial outside the Surf Ballroom in Clear Lake, Iowa. *Author*

getting off the bench to try and catch them when the van pulled out of the parking lot and vanished.

A wave of nostalgia and sadness washed over me. They reminded me of my own family many years ago. We did a lot of traveling in a blue minivan in the early years, and later in a small motor home. We never missed stopping at a historical marker. Now my kids are grown and scattered all over the country. Those precious years pass much to quickly.

I turned back to look at the building behind me. "You're a historic old place," I mumbled. "I'm glad you still stand."

I reached out to touch the brick with my hand before walking around the perimeter of the Surf. There were several back and side doors. I read somewhere that Buddy, Ritchie, and the Big Bopper left out the back door and climbed into a waiting station wagon for the ride to the Mason City airport just a few miles away.

"Which door was it?" I wondered as I let my mind wander back several decades. I pictured them walking outside in the dark frigid Iowa winter and loading into a 1950s-vintage wagon. Someone laughed. Someone else complained about the cold. I could see Buddy in his long coat with a big fur collar and carrying a small bag that he throws into the back. He turns the coat collar up around his neck and jokingly shouts to the Big Bopper, "Get away from that door! I'm riding front seat!" as he darts past J. P. Richardson and slips through the open front passenger door. More laughter. Ritchie and Bopper climb in the back. Three doors slam shut, their echo bouncing through the cold air. Three young talented men working hard and beginning to enjoy real stardom. I want to warn them—"Stop! Wait . . . don't go!" I shout inside my mind. But they don't stop. They don't hear me. They aren't really there. And when they were here, I wasn't. I admit to having a very vivid imagination, and the movie reel that had just played out in my head left a sick feeling in the pit of my stomach.

It was now time to move on. The eagerness I had felt about driving out to the site of the crash was replaced with a feeling of dread. I felt as if I was about to attend a funeral for someone I cared deeply about rather than visit an empty crash site where people I have never met perished more than five decades ago. Should I go? Why? Was a visit to the site germane to the book I was writing? A visit wouldn't really change anything. Everyone already knows this story doesn't end well. And there are plenty of pictures of the site.

My phone rang. It was Arlene.

"Well? How's it going," she asked.

"I'm at the Surf." My voice cracked a bit and my eyes began to fill. I felt like telling her I had just watched three friends drive off to their death, and I couldn't stop them.

"Yeah?" Arlene asked. The tone of her voice in that one word tells me she understood that I was upset. "Are you going to be okay?"

"Of course," I said in my most masculine voice. "It's just an old building. Why wouldn't I be okay?"

"I know, but I see what this has all come to mean to you," she replied. "Buddy has been in your life for many months, Gary."

I needed to change the subject or I was going to break down. "You should see this town, Arlene. It's charming and the lake is beautiful. We could live here if it were closer to a major airport."

"I'm sorry I didn't come with you," she said, ignoring my observation about Clear Lake. "I should've come along."

"I love being with you, but no. I realize I need to do this alone. I'd be embarrassed if you were with me." There was a long pause while I tried to regain my composure. "I need to vent this . . . whatever this is. I don't understand how I got . . . how I ended up *here*. We went to a concert with your mom. Now I'm in Clear Lake, Iowa. That song . . . I don't know." My voice cracked again. "Here I am months later on a tour of old Iowa ballrooms. Now I'm going to take a walk into a muddy cornfield. Why? This is nuts. Why should I care about any of this like I do?"

"Gary, come home. You're very tired," said Arlene. "We'll talk about it tonight and we'll get out the calendar and find a time when I can go with you. I miss you."

"I miss you too and I'll see you in a few hours," I replied. "I have one more stop to make, then I'll head for home." I took a deep sigh and exhaled slowly and softly.

"Are you sure you want to go there?" Arlene knows me so well. She knows me better than I know myself.

"Yeah. I'll make it quick and head for home," I lied. She knew I would linger, ponder. A quick visit to the crash site was never in the cards.

"Okay. I love you," she replied. "Don't text while driving."

"I love you, too. And I would never text while driving!" I laughed.

I clicked my phone off and was about to put my car into drive and head north when I remembered I had an app on my iPhone called "Roadside America." I pulled it up and clicked it for local attractions. Up popped "Buddy Holly Crash Site." I clicked on the map and it gave me directions straight there.

Chapter 31

And black nights

I was off and running. I just needed to follow the magic blue line 5.3 miles until there was no more blue line. A few minutes later I ran out of blue line and stopped.

I was there. But . . . where was I?

On my left was a farmhouse. A man in a blue T-shirt was using a weed-whacker along his fence. He looked up and I smiled and waved. He pointed to the other side of the road. I turned and looked to see a cornfield with an old barbed-wire fence running away from the road. I looked back at the man and did my best to ask a question with the puzzled look on my face. He lifted his arm and pointed again down the fence line.

He'd seen this movie before.

I pulled over and parked on the side of the road and climbed out of my car. I felt awkward, but walked across the road. "Hi there," I said in my friendliest voice.

"Just follow that fence line about half a mile. You'll see it," he replied.

I extended my hand and he took it. "I'm Gary Moore. I'm an author." I had no idea why I told him I was an author.

"Keith Mastre," he responded, still gripping my hand tightly. "I'm a farmer." He smiled. "Retired."

Keith Mastre. Iowa farmer. Retired. *Author*

"Is he mocking me?" I wondered. "How long have you lived here, Keith?" I asked.

"All my life." The retired Iowa farmer turned to his right and pointed to a house that was being rebuilt. "I was born and raised over there. When I married, my wife and I built this house," he continued, pointing to the home directly behind him.

"When I drove up you pointed across the road," I said.

He looked straight at me a few seconds—and I mean right in my eyes. "That's why you're here, right? Why else would you come down this road?"

Of course I knew exactly what he meant. "Yeah, I guess you're right," I answered. I looked back down the fence line. It was deathly quiet. "Did you live here the night of the crash?" I asked.

"Oh yeah," Keith said and nodded. "I was a freshman in high school. I was a fan of Buddy, but didn't get to go to the Surf that night. Farm chores," he explained with perhaps a twinge of regret in his voice. "The plan ended up about half a mile from here. Ours is as close as any other house, I guess. We didn't hear anything, though."

"Keith, do you remember what the weather was like that night?" I asked

"There was one heck of a snow squall that started after midnight," he answered. "It didn't last too long, though. That's what my dad said. Visibility was poor."

"How did you learn about the crash?" I inquired. "When did you hear about it?"

"It was the next morning. I got up to catch the late bus for school and people began showing up and turning into the field," he answered. "Police. Emergency vehicles. Dad walked a few yards out into the field. Said he could see what he thought was an airplane. That's all. We had no idea who was in it." Keith stopped talking and it was only then that I realized he was staring straight down that fence line as though he was looking for that plane even now.

"So you didn't go and take a look?"

"No," he replied quickly and firmly. "Dad wouldn't allow it. I'm glad now." Keith lowered his eyes and looked down at the ground. His emphasis on the word *now* made it clear to me he had not been as pleased with his dad's decision in 1959. "I hear from those who did go that it was an ugly mess. We learned in school that day what happened. We couldn't believe it happened in our town. All three of them," Keith continued. "Well four, including the pilot. They died here in Iowa. They almost died on my front lawn."

We both stood there, staring down that fence line as if we were watching the final events of that early February morning unfold all over again.

"There was no foul play," Keith offered. "You know, all the rumors about what happened in the plane? No one was shot. There was a snow squall, simple as that. My dad couldn't see through it, so imagine a pilot going over 150 miles an hour. What is he going to see?" Keith asked.

"A white blur?" I offered.

"Exactly."

"You know, the Weather Channel refers to this crash as one of the top 100 biggest weather moments in history," I said.

He didn't respond, and there really wasn't a need to answer. We both stared down the old fence line, a retired farmer and a stranger bound together by events that took place more than five decades earlier.

The wheels in my mind began to spin. I pictured men yelling to one another, but could not make out what they were saying. A police car pulled up, wheels spinning and the back end sliding from side to side in the snow-covered field. My heart began racing.

Keith interrupted the movie playing in my head. "A few days later, it was over. I thought it was back to being a cornfield one year and a bean field the next, but no." His voiced softened. "It had all changed." Keith looked down at his work boots and lifted the left one to look at the mud stuck to its sole.

"What . . . changed?" I asked.

"They started coming almost immediately," he answered. "They'd take a walk down that fence line, and for what? From all over the world they came. Every nationality. To see what? They still come from all over—fifty-plus years later, they are still coming." He furrowed his brow and looked at me as if wanting an explanation.

I didn't really have one. What was I going to say? That I hadn't really heard of Buddy Holly, but I went to a show in Cedar Falls and this guy named John who looks like Buddy played a song about Buddy and . . . and what? I decided to keep quiet.

"Look at you. You're here now. Can you tell me why?" Keith asked.

I shrugged. "No. Not really. I have asked myself that question over and over. I was even wondering that as I drove out here." I thought for a moment before continuing. "I'd like to say I'm here for my profession. I'm writing about it, but it's become . . . well, let's just say it's become something more than that." I turned to look back down the fence line. "So much more."

"See what I mean?" Keith continued. "It'll never be just a cornfield again." No elaboration was necessary.

"May I take your picture?" I asked, lifting my iPhone chest-high. "Assuming I ever finish this manuscript, maybe we can use it in the book. Would that be alright with you?"

"Sure," he answered. I snapped it quickly.

"When was the last time you walked down there, Keith?" I asked.

"Never."

The single word answer stunned me. "Wait. You've *never* walked down there? Not days after the crash as a high school student? Not ever?" I was not sure I believed him. He shook his head. I asked again. "You're telling me that since February 3, 1959, you have *never* walked the half-mile down the fence line to the crash site?"

"Right. That's what I'm telling you." He shot me a quizzical look as if wondering why I would doubt him.

I slowly shook my head. "People come from all over the world to this place and you have never walked across the road to see it." I think I said those words out loud more for my own understanding than anything else. I shrugged and looked back down the fence line. "Okay, well. I'm going."

"Of course you are going. That's why you came. So go take a look and let me get back to all my work," he said with a wide and warm Iowa smile.

I turned to walk away and then turned back. "Want to come with me, Keith?" I asked, my eyebrows raised high in the faint hope he might say yes.

He was silent for a couple seconds. "No. You go. I have work to do. There's nothing there but sadness." He made a brushing motion with his hands as if to shoo me away.

I thanked him for his kindness and turned and walked across the country road between Keith's home and the infamous field. He lived here and had never visited the site, but I was being drawn to it. I felt it. I couldn't *not* go—even if I tried to resist. But drawn there by what? A song?

I turned back and spotted Keith on his garden tractor heading for his house. I looked at my car. "Should I just climb in, turn the key, and leave?" I wondered aloud. No. I had to take the walk. What was I waiting for? Why was I stalling? I think I was looking for a reason not to go.

I took a deep breath and walked down into the ditch and back up the other side and entered the cornfield at the fence line. The fence was made of old barbed wire, knee high in a few spots and lying on the ground in others.

It had rained off and on all day and was beginning to drizzle again. Judging by the look of the old rusted wire and mixture of rusty steel and old wooden posts, they had been here a long time. Did they date from the time of the crash? Was this the original fence and a lifeless witness to the stars that fell from the sky shortly after midnight on February 3, 1959?

I reached down and touched the barbed wire as though I was touching something important . . . something precious.

I was wearing blue jeans a black T-shirt and, unfortunately, sandals. I took the first couple of steps and I sank ankle-deep in black Iowa mud. I turned to look back at Keith, but he was gone. A shiver of embarrassment coursed through me and I said aloud, "He thinks I'm nuts." I looked down the fence line and saw nothing but fence. I looked down and could not see my feet below the mud. "And he's right. I am."

"Is this the right place?" I wondered. The rain drops came down a little harder. I had read somewhere online that there was a marker . . . a large pair of glasses at the entrance to the field. I looked back. There are no glasses. Keith wouldn't have sent me on a wild goose chase, would he? Maybe I was entering from the other side of the field. I kept going.

I contemplated walking a few inches from the fence where there was some grass, but I was in thin sandals and the barbed wire was on the ground as much as it was strung between the fence posts. I was about to give it a try when I realized I hadn't had a tetanus shot in years. I decided

Keith Mastre and I stood on the edge of the country road staring down this old fence line (center distance). A little more than one-half mile from this point, the Beechcraft Bonanza came to rest against this very fence after cartwheeling across the field (from right to left), leaving a 570-foot debris field in its wake. *Author*

to stay in the mud. I pulled one foot out, put it in front, and watched as it sank into the ground as I yanked out the other and repeated the process. The mud especially liked my left sandal, which insisted on remaining behind each time I lifted my foot. I kept moving. The rain kept falling.

After struggling about one-quarter of a mile I stopped to study the lay of the land. Nothing ahead. I looked back toward my car. I couldn't even see it because of the the corn, which varied between knee- and waist-high. I drew a deep breath and exhaled. It took a lot of energy to wade (and that is really what I was doing—walking is a charitable description) through ankle-deep mud. A loud clap of lightning broke somewhere in the distance and a few seconds later the rumble of thunder reached my ears. The rain came down even harder. I was already soaked to the skin.

"Perfect!" I shouted in frustration. "This is just perfect!"

My sandals—at the beginning of my trek to the crash site. *Author*

I had to keep going. I yanked out my left foot and left my sandal behind. Again. I reached down to find it and slip it back on. The mud was the blackest and richest soil I had ever seen. I took a few more steps and said to myself, "It should be. It was fertilized with the lives of four young men." That odd thought really creeped me out.

What made me think of that?

I finally spotted something up ahead. It looked like flowers on a fence post maybe? I wasn't really sure. I turned and looked back toward the road, shook my head, and looked ahead once more. I alternated between walking (or rather, stumbling) and wading a few more minutes and then stopped dead in my tracks.

My pulse rate increased.

I'm here.

Chapter 32

Hey, Buddy . . .
Listen to me

Ahead was a small patch of land about ten feet by ten feet where the corn was not growing. There were two markers on the ground. One was a stainless steel guitar with three of the old 45-rpm records, one hit from each performer. On my right was an obviously separate stainless steel marker. It looked like wings with the name of Roger Peterson. The pilot.

I sucked in a breath and held it. The ground all around the markers for Buddy, Ritchie, and the Big Bopper was littered with a variety of items. Hotel keys, business cards, handwritten notes, framed letters, and plastic wrist bands in a variety of colors. There was also a CD and an assortment of guitar picks. I wanted to pick up some of the items to examine them, but felt it would be too disrespectful. These were gifts and mementos left by others and were not meant to be touched by me.

I looked southeast toward the airport but could see nothing but grain silos and corn as far as my eyes could see. The plane had been airborne for such a short time—five minutes . . . maybe six? The pilot within me began to reconstruct what happened and I began to feel sick. I could hear the roar of the Bonanza engine as it became louder and closer with each pulse-pounding second. Flight instructors drill into students the faith to

A close-up of the crash site memorial. *Author*

trust their instruments in limited or zero visibility. It's all you have when you have nothing else. Whether Roger was misreading his instruments as some suspect, or if (as I believe) he just lost control of his plane, slipped into a spiral, and was unable to recover, the plane struck the ground with throttle up at full power and rolled itself into a ball of aluminum and wire. The landing gear was up, and he was in a ninety-degree turn so close to the surface that his wing caught the ground. The plane cartwheeled.

"Stop!" I said aloud, snapping myself out of the ugly scene playing out inside my head.

I looked down at the markers. "I'm not here to be sad or to analyze what happened," I told myself. "Then why am I here?"

I looked around the field and felt the anxiety drain away. I was drawn there to celebrate the lives of Ritchie, the Big Bopper, Roger, and Buddy, not focus on their terrible deaths.

My mood changed quickly from sadness to joy. I pulled out my iPhone and began snapping pictures. Given all the water and mud it was easier said than done, but I did the best I could. My sense of joy increased and I clicked on "Hey, Buddy" on my iPhone and John Mueller began singing.

I was overwhelmed with emotion impossible to fully describe.

And then I did something totally out of character: I began to move. I rarely dance and then only when Arlene forces me. For only the second time in my life I felt the urge . . . no not urge . . . I felt compelled to dance! My feet began moving in the mud. My arms were outstretched, my eyes closed, my entire body moved and I realized I was celebrating the life and work of the incredible Buddy Holly and his companions, Ritchie Valens and J. P. "Big Bopper" Richardson. A few tears mixed with the summer rain and flowed down my cheeks and I laughed aloud! I felt so grateful for their legacy. I felt totally and completely blessed, feeling as though Buddy, Ritchie, the Big Bopper and Roger were dancing and laughing with me. I spun, I turned, I yelled! Mud splashed everywhere and I didn't care as I sang along with John.

"Hey Buddy rave on, and sing us a song, Baby won't you come out tonight . . ."

A self-portrait at the crash site memorial. *Author*

I must have looked like a member of some primitive tribe covered in mud and dancing around the campfire. I was totally and completely immersed in the moment. And then the song . . . stopped.

I slowly opened my eyes and looked around. The clouds had parted and the sun was beginning to shine. I smelled the clean rain-fresh Iowa air, filled with the aroma of organics.

I sank to my knees and began praying for those who had lost their lives in this field, for their family members, and for their friends.

I thanked God for bringing Buddy into my life through John Mueller.

I prayed that this site would only bring happiness and joy to others.

I also thanked God for the farmer who owned that field and that he would continue to allow the markers to remain and allow strangers to visit. In today's crazy world of litigation, I think it is a blessing to us all that he allows strangers from around the world to walk through his field to reach this first field of dreams.

I closed my prayers and stood. I tried to wipe the mud from my knees but it was useless. I looked at my mud-covered hands and tried to wipe them on my pants, but that was also a waste of time. I didn't care. I

The crash site memorial for pilot Roger Peterson. *Author*

laughed instead, screaming as loud as I could, "Who would ever believe this?"

A rush of gratitude surged through me. I needed to tell John Mueller. I cleaned off my fingers as best as I could, grabbed my iPhone, composed a quick e-mail, and attached a picture of me at the site.

John,

I'm standing here, all alone, ankle deep in the mud. It is raining and I'm listening to you sing "Hey, Buddy" on my iPhone. I'm touched deeply and still cannot figure out why. I do not understand why I am here at this moment but I know I am grateful to you, my new buddy John, for this experience.

Thank you.

Gary

I pressed send and looked around. The sky was already half clear and the sun was shining bright. A light breeze brushed by my face and I smiled. Was that Buddy passing by? I took one last look around and said my goodbyes. I could never have anticipated this experience. And how could I ever describe it without sounding . . . well . . .

I missed Arlene. It was time to walk back to my car and make the seven-hour drive home to Illinois.

I was completely exhausted by the time I reached my car parked along that country road. "Hey. It's done," I said into my iPhone.

"It's done? You sound happy!" she replied.

"How did all this happen to me?" I asked. "I am absolutely overjoyed. I can't explain it."

Arlene laughed. "Well, you better figure out how to explain it or this whole journey has been a colossal waste of time!"

"Where are you now?" I asked.

"Just packing the car," she responded.

The crash site entrance (on the opposite side from where I entered), with an oversized pair of Buddy's iconic glasses. *Author*

"Take your time and I'll catch up to you. We can grab a bite in Iowa City. I love you, Arlene."

"I love you, too. Hurry to Iowa City. I want to hear all about it!"

I followed the road around the field. I had been right. I entered from the wrong side. Along the side of the road sat a huge pair of black glasses marking the proper entrance to *The Field*. Who was responsible for them? The farmer? The community? It was so clever, a unique tribute to Buddy and the three other young men who died there.

The final words of the song rang in my head:

"Hey, Buddy . . . I'll see you on down the line."

Chapter 33

Something touched me deep inside

"**Gary!** You'll never guess why I am calling!" said the excited voice through my phone.

Tris Coburn is my literary agent and friend. He is normally a pretty relaxed guy, but something had him energized and I could not imagine what that might be.

"Hey Tris, what's up?" I asked.

"You have a nine o'clock appointment tomorrow morning to interview Don McLean!" Tris replied.

"What?" His announcement didn't completely register.

"Yes, you heard right!" Tris confirmed. He had to be telling me the truth. I had never heard him so excited.

"How'd you pull this off?" I asked.

"That doesn't matter. Can you do this at nine?" he asked.

"Sure. Yes . . . of course I can!" I paused. "Nine in what time zone?"

"Nine eastern," he answered. "McLean is on the east coast. So nine in the morning his time, so that is what? Eight your time?"

"Yes. Eight my time—wait, is it ten?" I was getting nervous and excited. The last thing I wanted to do was blow this opportunity because I had the time zone wrong! "No. Eight is right. Eight central time. Will he call me?" I asked.

"No," Tris said firmly. "You call him. He was very clear that you will have only twenty minutes, so you need to be prepared. Do you know what to ask?"

"Yes . . . No . . . Well, sort of. I think I want to ask him about Buddy's enduring impact. The opening lyrics of 'American Pie' certainly indicate Buddy had a huge impact on him," I responded.

"This guy is an international megastar, so be careful," warned Tris. "Be prepared and be on time."

"Wait Tris!" I said, suddenly locked in the grip of worry. "Ted said they would be sending the manuscript off this week to be printed for the media ARCs (Advanced Reading Copy). I better call and see if we can even do this."

"What? You have to be kidding me," my agent replied. "Of course you can. Ted will understand and wait for this! An interview like this is worth waiting for!" Tris insisted.

I hung up the phone and was dialing Savas Beatie to share the news before I even realized I didn't say thank you or goodbye to Tris.

"Good morning, Savas Beatie. This is Kim, how may I help you?" said the pleasant female voice on the other end of the call.

"Is Ted available?" I asked with excitement.

"I'm sorry. He's on another call," Kim replied. "Can I take a message?"

"No!" I yelled into the phone before assuming better control of my enthusiasm. I needed to dial it down several notches. "No message." I thought for a moment. "Kim, this is Gary Moore. Is Sarah available?"

"Hello Mr. Moore. Just a moment, please."

A few seconds later the familiar voice of my publisher's Marketing Director clicked onto the line. "This is Sarah."

"Stop the presses!" I yelled. (That was so much fun to say!)

Sarah laughed. "Hi Gary. Stop what presses?"

"Are the ARCs being printed?" I asked.

"Hmm. I can check but I don't think quite yet," Sarah answered. "Why?"

"Tris arranged to have Don McLean speak to me in the morning."

"Wow! That's great, Gary!" exclaimed Sarah. "Let me get Ted off his call. He'll want to hear this."

I was only on hold for a matter of seconds before another familiar voice came on the line. "How in the world did you manage this?" Ted Savas, Managing Director of Savas Beatie, demanded.

"Tris arranged it," I replied proudly. "Now we need him to get Sir Paul on the phone and we're all set!" By Sir Paul, of course, I was referring to Paul McCartney.

"No kidding," Ted replied. "Is Tris really working on McCartney?"

"Yeah. Well, he's sent letters and made phone calls, but there's been no response," I admitted. "I doubt it will happen, but we'll see. But I didn't think he would get McLean!"

"McLean is better anyway," Ted said. "If he was only going to get one, McLean is the one to get for this book. What time are you scheduled to talk?"

"Nine tomorrow morning," I answered.

"Nine . . . Nine where?" asked Ted.

"Stop it!" I laughed. "Nine in the morning my time, so eight his time." I paused. "Wait . . . Oh man. I better call Tris back. No—it's nine a.m. Eastern Standard Time so eight Central Time. Everyone needs to stop asking me or I will screw this up!"

Ted laughed. "Boy, Gary, be sure you're right!"

"I know, I know . . ." I assured him before hanging up. I took a deep breath before shouting, "Oh no!" Within five minutes I had hung up on both my agent and my publisher without saying goodbye.

*   *   *

I tossed and turned all night. "What time did Tris say to call? I cannot get this wrong."

It was 4:11 a.m. and I had been checking the clock next to my bed at least twice an hour since my head touched the pillow. My conversation with Tris and Ted kept replaying in me head.

I have to go to sleep!

*   *   *

"Don't you have an interview this morning?" Arlene called out from her closet.

I sat straight up in bed. "What time is it?"

Arlene peeked around the closet door. "Seven. Why? Are you late?"

"Seven here is eight there, right? I'm supposed to call now?" I threw off the covers and turned to climb out of bed.

Arlene laughed and put her hand over her mouth as she stepped out of the closet. "I can hear it now! 'Is it eight a.m. his time or eight a.m. my time, which is nine a.m. for him.' You were mumbling something like that in your sleep all night long!" I leaped to me feet. "Slow down!" Arlene chuckled. "Last night you said to call him at eight our time. He is expecting your call at nine his time. You have a full hour."

"Are you sure?"

"Yes, I'm sure," she replied. "Calm down." Arlene disappeared into the bathroom and began brushing her teeth. I followed her.

She removed her toothbrush from her mouth. "What's going on?" she asked. "You don't get nervous. You're only talking to some musician." Arlene stuck the toothbrush back in her mouth.

"Some musician?" I answered. "Are you kidding? Don McLean wrote the song that defined the musical movement of the times! I didn't follow the music very closely, but I loved 'American Pie.' Who didn't?"

Arlene walked over and gave me a hug. "Get over it. Just call him and have a conversation with him. No big deal. I bet he's nervous now and is telling his wife that an author is going to call." Arlene smiled. "You think?"

"No!" She had to be kidding, right?

*   *   *

"Mr. McLean?" I asked the voice who answered my call.

"Yes."

I recognized the voice from one word. "My name is Gary Moore, and—"

The composer of "American Pie" interrupted me before I could finish a single sentence. "What's your book about?"

"Buddy Holly—but it's not a biography. It's about his ongoing and enduring influence. I've been interviewing people around the country who are explaining to me that—"

"Who? Who are you talking to?" McLean asked with a voice of authority.

My heart jumped inside my chest. "Mostly everyday people, really. Librarians to radio station owners to Bobby Vee. I spoke with a young graduate student who has a picture of Buddy tattooed on her back! Can you believe it?" I laughed. Don did not.

"I have someone tattooed on my back, too," Don replied softly. I was dying to ask who, but he kept talking. "Here is what you need to know about Buddy," Don began. "We have this distorted notion. We think we can reach back and touch Buddy Holly because of video, YouTube, and such. People today are like, Buddy this and Buddy that. Stars who died in the fifties are like Hula Hoops or something from Wham-O, you know what I mean? A fad. Once we were done we tossed them away. Do you understand? The British . . . the English groups were the only ones who are remembered. They came out in the early sixties and everyone thought it was something new—but it wasn't. It was actually music inspired by Buddy's style and in a few cases, it was actually Buddy's songs they were playing. The British had grasped Buddy's style and made it their own. Americans loved it when they did and acted as if they had not heard it before, but they had. They didn't recognize their own music! When you heard the early Beatles, you were hearing Buddy Holly. How did the Americans not get it?"

He was right. We embraced The Beatles, the Stones, and other British groups and treated them as if they invented Rock & Roll. In fact, they were not shy about telling us that it was Buddy and his influence they were using and imitating. Listen to interviews with John Lennon and Paul McCartney. Both former Beatles talked about Buddy and his influence often, but the American public didn't really "hear" what they were saying. It's as if we had collective amnesia. As if we wanted to believe this musical style was invented somewhere else.

"I say this," continued McLean, "not in an egotistical way, but it was my song. It was 'American Pie' that began bringing Buddy back. Buddy Holly biographer John Goldrosen says it. He had trouble getting his book published originally, but when 'American Pie' came out, it changed everything. Because of 'American Pie,' Buddy is back where he should be."

What he was saying was fascinating. Someone once told me that a business "expert" is someone with a briefcase who flies in from somewhere else on a plane. Was the same principle at work here? Did we believe that "the British invasion" music was so good that it could not have originated in the USA? It had to come from some outside "expert"? To be that good, it had to arrive here on a plane with someone carrying a guitar case? Images of The Beatles arriving in America in New York City waving to adoring fans filled my head.

"My memories of Buddy's death are different," McLean began again. Was I detecting a bit of anger in his voice? "I remember no one gave a shit. Back then, you faded fast. I don't think Buddy was treated well by the Crickets, who had left him, nor was he treated fairly by Norman Petty."

McLean was referring to Buddy's first manager and producer. They split in 1958. McLean's discourse was a potential minefield and an area I really wanted to avoid. Opinions differ greatly in this area between those who knew and loved Buddy. I decided to avoid further discussion on this.

McLean continued. "Money was withheld to make Buddy tow the line. That's why he was on the Winter Dance Party tour to begin with," McLean stated emphatically.

Buddy historian Bill Griggs has a very different view and opinion on the subject. But this was not an important part of the story I was trying to write, so I decided to avoid it altogether. Everyone has an opinion.

"Have you read the Goldrosen book?" Don asked.

"No," I answered. "I have it, but I have purposely not read it yet. I don't want to be influenced by it. I'm not writing a history book or biography. I'll read it once I'm done writing this."

Don didn't comment directly on my reasoning. "You should know more about this subject," he chastised. "You should have read the Goldrosen book."

How could he possibly fathom what I know or don't know? I wondered. I needed to stay focused on McLean.

"I fell in love with Buddy in 1957," he continued. I wasn't asking any questions. He was just telling a fascinating story and I was listening and writing as fast as I was able. "I tried to buy glasses like his when I was twelve. I wanted to learn to play the guitar like Buddy. I lived in New Rochelle, New York. I was a paperboy, which was the only other job I have ever had besides being a musician. I communed with his photos and music.

"He married Maria Elena in 1958 and moved to New York. He'd go down to Washington Square and listen to the 'folkies.' At that point he was already being left behind. People on the street didn't recognize him but the folk musicians did. They would gather around and talk to him, ask him questions about his music and guitar techniques."

People on the street didn't recognize Buddy in 1958? That would be really odd if it were 2010 (with our hundreds of television channels, YouTube, and the Internet). Musicians are much more visible and recognizable today. Where would the average fan see Buddy in 1959? Other than in a magazine or maybe an occasional newspaper, they would have to catch him on TV—on Ed Sullivan, Arthur Murray, and American Bandstand, and only then for a few minutes on each show. And how many homes had TVs back then? Were people already forgetting him in 1958, or was it because he was not as recognizable as today's musicians? Most people say Buddy was at the top of his career when he died in early 1959. Don seemed to be saying Buddy was already on his way out.

"I was cutting open my stack of papers to be delivered. That's how I learned about his death," Don continued. "I was devastated. I didn't realize how deeply it impacted me until years later. I wanted to write a song about America and it all surfaced. That song launched me into the stratosphere and re-launched Buddy with me. When you hear 'American Pie' on the radio today, it's often back to back with 'Peggy Sue' or 'Not Fade Away.'

"Buddy got more publicity in the six months after 'American Pie' came out than he did in his entire career," announced the famous voice on the other end of the phone. "It's almost as if there has been a channel open between Buddy and me, but here's the thing to remember about Buddy: he cut about sixty tracks then died when he was only twenty-two. His songs were hits. Hits! It's hard to point to anybody who wrote that many songs, all different styles, and had so many hits! That's amazing. The quantity and versatility of styles . . . Buddy's songs . . . they were homemade. Buddy was amazing. I don't think McCartney, Lennon, or anyone can touch him. It's also amazing how quickly the public tossed him aside."

Don paused. I glanced at my prepared list of questions. I had yet to ask the first one and was opening my mouth to do so when he said, "I hope all of this helps you," and hung up. The interview was over. Don McLean had left the building; well, at least the phone call.

I exhaled and felt as though I had been holding my breath throughout the entire interview. I wanted to ask him about John Mueller, whether he had ever heard John's song "Hey, Buddy," and so much more, but Don McLean was gone. I'll send him a copy of the finished book so he can see how his interview fits into it. I am thankful that he took the time to share his thoughts with me.

Chapter 34

Hey, Buddy . . . We'll see you on down the line

In Rock & Roll terms, Buddy's body of work is not that large. He was only in the professional limelight for about eighteen months. Considering that limited length of time, his work can also be considered rather voluminous. Buddy's songs are extensively covered by other artists. Some artists who have performed his songs include The Beatles, the Rolling Stones, Linda Ronstadt, and James Taylor, just to name a few. Don McLean's "American Pie" is replete with Buddy connections, and of course "Hey, Buddy," John Mueller's personal tribute, is all about the legend. Buddy's songs have been featured or used in movies and video games. The Buddy Holly Center in Lubbock is dedicated to his short but intense life. A statue and a street named after him and another after The Crickets also graces his hometown. The Buddy Holly Story is the name of both a movie and an ongoing Broadway-style musical production that plays worldwide. Buddy and his music live on. If you are aware of him and pay any attention at all, Buddy Holly is everywhere.

Celebrities from Sir Paul McCartney to Graham Nash, Bobby Vee and countless others admit that Buddy deeply and profoundly influenced and impacted their lives and their music. I'm not a celebrity and certainly

Left to right: John Mueller, Donna Ludwig (Ritchie Valens wrote and named his famous song "Donna" after her), Ritchie's sisters Connie and Irma Valenzuela (maiden name used for both), and Ray Anthony, who portrays Ritchie on stage with John. *John Mueller*

---

not distinguished in any meaningful way, but my name can also be added to that (growing) list.

Despite all of his accomplishments and the numerous tributes paid to the young man from Lubbock, what strikes me is the simple fact that Buddy grew up like me, and maybe like you, too. I have spent the better part of the last year talking to people about Buddy, and a common thread stands out: people everywhere did, and still do, relate to Buddy. Not Buddy the legend or Buddy the songwriter, but Buddy the young man from Lubbock. He reminds us of the kid next door or even more intimately, he reminds us of ourselves.

American kids idolized and adored The Beatles, but did they ever really relate to John, Paul, George, or Ringo in a personal and intimate way? Did Paul remind anyone of their next-door neighbor? Buddy was from small town America. He attended church. He was a Cub Scout. He stole trash can lids from his neighbors and stacked them at the end of the

Grammy winner Tommy Allsup (left), Buddy's guitarist on the Winter Dance Party tour in 1959, and John Mueller (right) in a Best Western in Tennessee in 2000. Tommy was originally scheduled to make the flight with Buddy to Fargo, North Dakota, but a coin flip with Ritchie Valens in the back of the Suf Ballroom determined otherwise. *John Mueller*

street because he thought it was funny. He was . . . typical. His report cards don't reflect genius any more than most of ours did. He grew up in a very modest ranch-style home in a neighborhood a lot like mine and maybe a lot like yours. Buddy Holly could have been Ron McIntosh, Jeff Frederickson, Dan Cote, or Greg Kunde, the young musicians I grew up with . . . or even Gary Moore. The more I learned, the more I realized I am drawn to Buddy not because of his extraordinary accomplishments, but because he was an ordinary kid who made it big but never forgot who he was and where he was from.

So Buddy Holly raves on in the minds and hearts of his fans, young and old, all over the globe. Unlike those who followed in his musical footsteps in the Rock & Roll tsunami that blew in after his death, Buddy didn't die of a drug overdose. He didn't throw up and choke on his own vomit in someone's backseat. He wasn't killed while drunk behind the wheel of an Italian sports car, and he didn't take his own life. Buddy never advocated free sex or drugs. But he was without question an inventor and pioneer of Rock & Roll. Buddy died aboard a plane that he

Hello,

My name is Eleanor. I am 7.
I am at the Winter dance
Party with my Sister Greta,
who is 4. We love your
music and we are Very excited
for the show. Good luck!
Eleanor
Kernkamp
GRETA
KERNKAMP
P.S. I hope you
play Peggy Sue.
Eleanor

Please sing Chantilly
Lace, Greta

A fan letter written to John Mueller (right) from 7-year-old Greta, with a drawing by her little sister (facing page).

John Mueller

chartered in an attempt to get to his destination with enough time to do his laundry. Buddy was out of clean socks and underwear.

Buddy Holly never grew old. He is as we knew him the last time we saw him. At the pinnacle of his career and popularity, he is unchangeably locked in love with his new bride and looking forward to building his recording studio and making a tremendous impact with his music.

Ask any Buddy Holly fan what comes to mind when he or she hears his name, and the answer is always the name of a song, THE black glasses, or the day the music died. None of these are the first thing that leap into my mind.

BUDDY HOLLY   BIG BOPPER   Ritchie Valens

BY Greta

I think of John Mueller and his moving tribute to a man he never met but who he knows so intimately that his every move causes Buddy's fans, friends, and family to feel as though Buddy is alive and onstage. I know in my heart and soul that Buddy approves of and appreciates John's words, the music, and the sentiment.

I think about how Buddy's first thought of what to do with his first royalty check was not to buy a car or go on vacation, but to use the money to purchase new pews for his church in Lubbock, Texas.

I think about my day in an Iowa cornfield, ankle-deep in mud, dancing and crying for joy while feeling a real connection with someone I have never met. It was unlike anything I have ever experienced.

I think of Don McLean's question in "American Pie."

I think about how my pursuit of Buddy Holly, my new buddy John, and Tim's and Jim's relentless mission to help me discover the music I missed and understand the actions of my generation have forever changed the way I look at music.

McLean asks, "Do you believe in Rock & Roll?"

I now answer, "Yes. Yes I do."

But above all, I think of a little brown-eyed girl in a cotton summer dress holding her father's hand with one of her own while using the other

John Mueller enters the original Eagles Ballroom (now called Madrigrano's Marina Shores) in Kenosha, Wisconsin, one of the few remaining original ballrooms from the 1959 Winter Dance Party tour. The photo was snapped by John's drummer Mark Micklethwaite. *John Mueller*

to shade her eyes from the Iowa sun that sparkles through her blonde hair. She is forever looking up at the planes high overhead. Her thoughts are not of death or tragedy, but of a handsome young Texas gentleman sporting sunglasses and tuning his guitar while sitting on a freezer in a ballroom kitchen in Waterloo, Iowa.

My journey has come to its inevitable end. My mother-in-law introduced me to the late, great Buddy Holly through my new buddy John Mueller and his timeless song. Because of this pursuit, I discovered an entire decade of music I had ignored. My evening at the Winter Dance Party triggered this journey. I have found a part of me I did not know existed.

I hear the melody of the chorus of "Hey, Buddy" in my head and feel the words in my heart.

John Mueller inside Norman Petty's famous studio in Clovis, New Mexico, where much of the video for "Hey, Buddy" was shot. *John Mueller*

Hey, Buddy . . . Rave On and sing us a song
Baby, won't you come out tonight
We're all looking for someone to love down here
You help us make it through these blue days and black nights

May God bless and keep you, Buddy. Thank you for your music, for the excitement, and for the enthusiasm you still generate. And thank you for the man you remain, frozen in time, forever twenty-two, in love with your wife.

Rave On.

An Interview with Author Gary W. Moore

Q. At first blush Hey Buddy *appears to be a very different book than your first effort,* Playing with the Enemy—*a music legend versus baseball and World War II. But in many ways they are very similar.*

A. They are. I think readers of my first book will realize very quickly that both are laden with emotion—and of course they are, because I am an emotional guy and don't pretend that I am not. My journey that led to *Playing with the Enemy* began with a long conversation with my father right before he died. I was overwhelmed with desire to discover who my dad was and write about the baseball career and incredible experiences I never knew he had. And it all took place during a much simpler time in America.

Q. And your "pursuit" in Hey Buddy *was triggered by a single event at a concert.*

A. Yes, that's right. Instead of hearing my dad tell me a story, John Mueller told me a story through his song "Hey, Buddy." That was it. I was hooked. I was captivated by the song, by the lyrics, by the music that evening—and by Buddy himself.

Q. So would it be fair to say you didn't really pick the subject matter. Rather, the subject matter picked you?

A. I wasn't a fan and knew very little about Buddy Holly, but one night, through the words of a song written about Buddy but not by him, he reached out through John Mueller at the Gallagher Bluedorn Performing Arts Center in Cedar Falls, Iowa, and seized my heart. I walked into that theater dreading the performance and left feeling compelled to write a book. How do you explain that to anyone?

Q. Early in the book your wife Arlene comments about your "obsessive tendencies." Care to comment?

A. (Laughing) Well, you can call it a gift or a curse, and my opinion changes daily as to which it is. Things catch my eye or ear and seize my mind and heart that other people usually ignore. She calls it an obsession. I call it focus. (More laughter.) Arlene's description is closer to the truth. Once something interests me I don't let go. Arlene is the perfect example. We've been married for more than thirty-five years!

Q. You weren't a fan of Holly or of rock music in general. Did that make the research difficult for you?

A. No, because I felt compelled to do it and this is not a scholarly Buddy Holly biography. Although I performed plenty of what you could call "research," my efforts were largely focused on interviews. It was a labor of love and a discovery of myself. The more I learned, the more I had to know. I enjoyed each and every minute of it, and now that I am finished I cannot imagine not having done it.

Q. Are you a Buddy Holly fan now?

A. Big time. I have fallen in love with Buddy's music and have deep admiration and respect for his creativity, drive, and determination. What that young man accomplished in such a short time is nothing short of breathtaking. His influence on so much that followed is palpable, and if you pay attention, Buddy is still with us wherever you look and listen. I want to add that I am also a big time fan of John Mueller. He is a good man and a great talent.

Q. Tell me what was it like interviewing Don McLean. That was quite a coup.

A. It was, and it was a surreal experience. I spent hours preparing questions, even though I was told I would only have twenty minutes. But I didn't get to ask him a single one! I called Don and he just began talking. It was obvious he was offering a lot of valuable information that would have answered many of my questions anyway, so I just let it flow. When he finished he just hung up. Throughout I was typing like a mad man to capture every word. Talking with the composer of "American Pie" was an amazing experience and I feel privileged to have had the opportunity.

Q. Don says his song resurrected Buddy Holly. Do you agree?

A. I absolutely agree. "American Pie" is brilliant, and it cemented Buddy into the public consciousness like nothing else ever could or ever will.

Q. You wrote very little about Buddy's wife, Maria Elena Holly. That surprised me. Why not?

A. I really wanted to do a lot more with Maria Elena. I contacted her and we spoke twice on the phone about the possibility of an interview. Unfortunately, we just couldn't get together and I ran out of time.

Q. Is it fair to conclude that, since Hey Buddy *is not a biography but your personal journey to discover how Buddy continues to affect others, her participation was not really required?*

A. (Sigh) I guess you could say that. I really wanted to interview her and I'm sure she would have added a lot to the story. I'm also certain that after five decades she gets more than a little tired of being asked many of the same questions. I respect her privacy. Let's leave it at that.

Q. Other than Buddy's widow, who else do you wish you could have interviewed?

A. Above all, I would have loved to talk with Buddy. I also tried to arrange something with Sir Paul McCartney. He loved Buddy's music and credits Buddy with a lot of inspiration for his own writing and The Beatles. I often wonder if he has heard Mueller's "Hey, Buddy" and what he thinks of it. A conversation with Buddy's brothers Larry and Travis would have been useful, but like Maria Elena I think they have had enough after all this time and I respect their privacy. After they read the book and see it is very positive and very different than anything else out there, maybe they will agree to have a conversation. I would sure enjoy that.

Q. It's really surprising that Keith Mastre, the Iowa farmer who lived right at ground zero, had never visited the crash site. That seems incredible. Looking back, do you believe him, and if so, why do you think he never did?

A. Oh I absolutely believe him. He was looking me in the eye and he was telling me the gospel truth. Keith is a really sincere guy, and his answer floored me, too. But I take him at his word. He said there is nothing there "but sadness." I think that sums it up. He didn't need the experience. I did.

Q. Tell me something you discovered about Buddy that surprised you.

A. Buddy's deep faith surprised me. He didn't live the "rock star life" we have come to expect with the other stars who followed in his footsteps. He lived a life that was reflective of his beliefs and for that alone, Buddy has my undying respect. Think about it. He used his first royalty check to buy pews for his church! I don't think you will discover Keith Richards saying anything remotely similar in his new memoir.

Q. Tell me something you found out about John Mueller that surprised you.

A. That's easy. John is so much like Buddy! He is humble, respectful, and not at all absorbed by the adulation of his fans. Of course I never met Buddy, but when Buddy's friends describe him, it never fails to strike me that they are also describing John. It's sort of spooky when you think about it.

Q. You didn't take a photograph of the kitchen at the Electric Park Ballroom where photographer Dick Cole snapped that iconic image of Buddy tuning his guitar (the same one used on the dust jacket). Why not?

A. My publisher asked me the same question! I walked back into the kitchen to do just that, but it had been completely updated and changed. There was no freezer like the one in the picture, and no way to tell where it once sat. But you know what? In some dump or landfill in the Waterloo area is an famous old freezer buried among the trash. Wish I knew where to dig!

Q. Bill Griggs was really helpful to you in preparing this book. How is he doing? How's his health?

A. He was indeed helpful and I am very thankful. Bill is a quite ill but a real trooper. When I talk with him he is always positive and upbeat. Hopefully he will be around for long, long time.

Q. You didn't set out to write about the infamous plane crash in any depth— but you did. What changed your mind?

A. I wanted a happy uplifting book, so writing about the horrifying final moments Buddy and those other young men experienced in that little plane was the last thing I wanted to do. I didn't think it was reflective of the story I set out to pen.

Q. Was it Barb Dwyer's call?

A. Yes. If Barb had not called me back and claimed that "the truth has never come out about that flight," and "the truth has never been told," the story would have written itself very differently. I tried to ignore her claim but I just couldn't. How can an author ignore that? So as a former pilot and charter service owner, I started investigating, read the reports, studied the type of plane and its characteristics, and talked at length with a retired NTSB expert who spent his career evaluating aviation disasters. As it turned out, there was quite a bit to write germane to the story. I have no doubt the Dwyers are wonderful people and I wish them nothing but the best, but I think they owe the families and fans an explanation about this so-called untold "truth." They are no longer young, and if there is something to say, they should say it.

Q. You did something I don't think any other author has done—called on Jerry and Barb Dwyer to either prove they have the plane wreckage or admit that they don't and end the speculation. Why did you do that and what do you hope to achieve by doing it?

A. I really hesitated doing that, but finally decided I had no choice. It came down again to that statement Barb made to me—over and over. She was so adamant about it. And they have been telling people for decades they have the plane and can prove it. OK—prove it. Show us the plane, let experts examine it, and let's get the true story out for the history books. Let's put all the conspiracies and other nonsense to rest. I think the CAB report is dead-on accurate, and so does the expert I consulted. I hope the chapters dealing with the crash correct some lingering inaccurate information. As I say in the book, sometimes it just is what it is.

Q. Ted Savas, the managing director of the house that published your book, grew up in Mason City just eight miles from the crash site, but he has never been there. Now he lives 2,000 miles away in California. Have you ever asked him why?

A. I did actually ask him that. Ted and I are good friends, so we talked for hours at all hours of the day and night about this book! His response is typical of many people who live around "famous" sites. He said, "I never really gave it much thought, and when I did, there was always tomorrow. And then I moved away." Sometimes you never visit your own backyard because you take what's there for granted. I knew a guy who grew up in San Antonio and never visited the Alamo!

Q. Has the crash site been accessible since the date of the accident?

A. From what I have learned, yes and no. From 1959 until about ten or fifteen years ago the site was not readily accessible because it was not well marked, and the exact location was not made known in a public sort of way. The Internet, GPS, and other advances, together with the ongoing influence and appeal of Buddy's music, increased the desire among fans to make the pilgrimage to the place the music died.

Q. I imagine you recommend that every Buddy Holly fan make that trip.

A. Absolutely. I found it incredibly moving, inspirational—even spiritual. I told Ted I look forward to visiting the site again and taking him with me. Hopefully when we do it will be with John Mueller and his acoustic guitar. We can play for Buddy.

Buddy Holly:
A Partial Timeline of a Remarkable Life

1936: September 7, Charles Hardin Holley is born to Ella and Lawrence Odell "L.O." Holley on Labor Day at the Holley's Sixth Street home in Lubbock.

1949: Buddy's first recording is "My Two-Timin' Woman," a Hank Snow song, which he sings into a wire recorder.

1954/55: Buddy, joined at various times by Bob Montgomery, Sonny Curtis, Larry Welborn, Don Guess and/or J. I. Allison, travels to Nesman Recording Studio in Wichita Falls to record a number of songs including: "Flower of My Heart," "Door to My Heart," "Soft Place in My Heart," "Gotta Get You Near Me Blues," "I Gambled My Heart, "Down the Line," "You and I Are Through," "Baby Let's Play House," and "Queen of the Ballroom."

February 13: Buddy and Bob Montgomery open for Elvis Presley at the Fair Park Coliseum in Lubbock.

October 14: At the Fair Park Coliseum, Buddy, Bob Montgomery, and Larry Welborn perform in a show featuring Bill Haley and The Comets and Jimmy Rodgers Snow.

October 15: Buddy, Bob Montgomery, and Larry Welborn open for Elvis at the Fair Park Coliseum.

October 28: Buddy, Bob Montgomery, and Larry Welborn open for headliner Marty Robbins at the Fair Park Coliseum. Eddie Crandall again watches Buddy's performance.

1956

January 23-25: Buddy negotiates a recording contract with Decca and a three-year songwriter's contract with Cedarwood Publishing Company.

February 8: Buddy's name is misspelled in Decca's contract, with the "e" inadvertently dropped from Holley. As a result, Buddy adopts the "Holly" spelling for his last name.

April 21: Billboard reviews "Love Me": "If the public will take more than one Presley or Perkins, this one stands a chance."

1957

January 22: Decca sends Buddy a letter informing him that his renewal option is not being exercised and his contract will expire on January 26, 1957.

February/March: Buddy is restricted from recording any of the songs that were done under his contract with Decca. A name is needed in order to release the new version of "That'll Be The Day." J. I. Allison searches through an encyclopedia under "Insects" in order to find a name for the band. They consider briefly, then discard "The Beetles" before selecting "The Crickets."

July 1: "Peggy Sue," "Oh Boy," "Listen To Me," and "I'm Gonna Love You Too" are recorded in Clovis, New Mexico.

August 2: Buddy Holly and The Crickets begin their first major tour at the Howard Theater in Washington, D.C. where "That'll Be The Day" is number two on the charts.

August 16-22: Buddy Holly and The Crickets perform at the Apollo Theater in New York City.

August 26: Buddy Holly and The Crickets perform "That'll Be The Day" on Dick Clark's American Bandstand in Philadelphia, Pennsylvania.

August 27: Buddy Holly and The Crickets appear on the Ted Steele Show in New York City.

August 30: The Alan Freed Holiday Show at the Paramount Theater in New York features Buddy Holly and The Crickets.

September 9: Buddy Holly and The Crickets join the Biggest Show of Stars for 1957 in Norfolk, Virginia.

September 21: Cash Box features a cover photograph of Buddy Holly and The Crickets pointing to a circled date of October 1, 1957. "That'll Be The Day" is expected to pass the one million mark in sales on this date. Two days later Billboard lists "That'll Be The Day" as the No. 1 best seller in stores.

November 27: Brunswick releases the album The Chirping Crickets.

December 1: Buddy Holly and The Crickets perform "That'll Be The Day" and "Peggy Sue" on The Ed Sullivan Show.

December 4-5: Buddy Holly and The Crickets return to Lubbock. Niki Sullivan leaves the group.

December 23: Buddy Holly and The Crickets are billed separately during the 12-day Alan Freed's Christmas Jubilee Show (also billed as the Holiday of Stars) at the Paramount Theater in New York City.

1958

January 8: Buddy Holly and The Crickets join America's Greatest Teenage Recording Stars tour in Charlotte, North Carolina.

January 25: Bob Thiele of Coral presents Buddy Holly and Norman Petty with the gold record for "Peggy Sue." The songs "Rave On" and "That's My Desire" are recorded at Bell Sound Studios in New York.

January 26: Buddy Holly and The Crickets perform "Oh Boy" on The Ed Sullivan Show in New York City.

January 28-29: Buddy Holly and The Crickets travel to Sydney, Australia for a six-day tour. *Variety* runs an article about the Honolulu show under the headline, "Rock n' Roll Reaches Hawaii & Makes Good," and describes "turn-away crowds."

February 20: Buddy Holly and The Crickets join The Big Gold Records Stars tour (informally known as The Florida Tour). Coral releases the album Buddy Holly, which includes the songs: "I'm Gonna Love You Too," "Peggy Sue," "Look at Me," "Listen to Me," "Valley of Tears," "Ready Teddy," "Everyday," "Mailman Bring Me No More Blues," "Words of Love (You're So Square) Baby I Don't Care," "Rave On," and "Little Baby."

February 28: Coral in England releases "Listen To Me/I'm Gonna Love You Too," and "Maybe Baby/Tell Me How." Buddy Holly and The Crickets and Norman and Vi Petty arrive in London to begin the 25-day tour of the United Kingdom.

March 14: Buddy Holly and The Crickets perform "Maybe Baby," which is broadcast live over the BBC's Off The Record TV show, and "I'm Gonna Love You Too" for a promotional advertisement for the show. During one of the group's evening performances at the Granada Theatre in Woolwich, London, Mick Jagger is reportedly among the members of the audience.

March 27: Buddy Holly and The Crickets join Alan Freed's Big Beat Show in Brooklyn, New York.

July 4: Buddy Holly and The Crickets, accompanied by Tommy Allsup and his dance band, perform for the Summer Dance Party tour.

July 8: During a performance at Electric Park in Waterloo, Iowa, Dick Cole asks Buddy to remove his glasses for a picture. Buddy replies: "I never have pictures made without my glasses."

August 15: Buddy and Maria Elena Santiago are married at the Holley home in Lubbock. Parents L.O. and Ella Holley, brothers Larry and Travis, sister Patricia and the spouses of his brothers and sister are in attendance, along with J. I. and Peggy Sue Allison and Joe B. Mauldin. The Hollys and the Allisons honeymoon for two weeks in Acapulco, Mexico.

September 10: A session for Waylon Jennings is produced by Buddy for his newly founded company Prism Records.

October 28: Buddy Holly and The Crickets appear on Dick Clark's American Bandstand on WFIL-TV in Philadelphia, Pennsylvania.

November 3: Buddy ends his business partnership with Norman Petty. J. I. Allison and Joe B. Mauldin decide to remain under Petty's management.

December 25: Buddy and Maria Elena spend Christmas with Buddy's family in Lubbock.

1959

January 20-22: Buddy, Tommy Allsup, Waylon Jennings, and Carl Bunch leave New York City and travel by train to Chicago to rendezvous with the other artists on the Winter Dance Party tour. From Chicago, the artists are scheduled to travel by bus on the tour route. Other performers include: Ritchie Valens, J. P. "Big Bopper" Richardson, Dion and The Belmonts, and Frankie Sardo.

January 23: The Winter Dance Party kicks off the tour with performances in Milwaukee, Wisconsin.

February 2: Buddy Holly, Waylon Jennings, and Tommy Allsup perform and serve as back-up musicians during the performance at the Surf Ballroom in Clear Lake, Iowa.

February 3: Shortly after the performance in Clear Lake, Buddy Holly, J. P. "Big Bopper" Richardson, and Ritchie Valens board a small aircraft chartered to take them to their next performance. The plane crashes just minutes after take-off, killing everyone aboard.

For a complete timeline of Buddy Holly's remarkable life, and for more information, please see www.buddyhollycenter.org

About the Author:

Gary W. Moore is a motivational speaker, an accomplished musician, a former pilot and flight charter service owner, and the award-winning author of *Playing with the Enemy: A Baseball Prodigy, World War II, and the Long Journey Home* (Savas Beatie, 2006; Penguin, 2008), soon to be a major motion picture. Gary has contributed to the Chicken Soup for the Soul series and has been featured in national publications, on syndicated radio, and on CNN, ABC, NBC, CBS, and Fox.

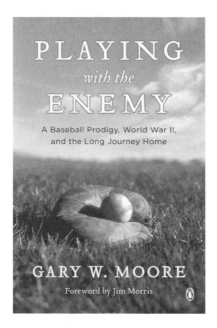

In bookstores and online–everywhere.

For more information, see www.heybuddybook.com